102 TOOLS
FOR TEACHERS & COUNSELORS TOO

By
MARY JOE HANNAFORD

Illustrated by
JOEY HANNAFORD

Revised/Reprinted 2001

Copyright © 1991 Mary Joe Hannaford
Printed with permission of the author by
mar*co products, inc.
1443 Old York Road
Warminster, PA 18974
1-800-448-2197

ISBN: 1-575-430-061

TABLE OF CONTENTS

INTRODUCTION 7

TO THE LEADER 9

HINTS TO FOLLOW 11

GROUP STRUCTURES 13

TOOLS FOR STARTING GROUPS 15

    Tool 1—Group Starters (K-Adult/Ages 5 and up) 17
    Tool 2—Discussion Starters (Grades 4-Adult/Ages 9 and up) 19

TOOLS FOR GROUP OR CLASSROOM MANAGEMENT 21

    Tool 3—Help (Grades K-4/Ages 5-9) 23
    Tool 4—Footsteps (Grades K-4/Ages 5-9) 24
    Tool 5—Grumpy Pillow (Grades K-4/Ages 5-9) 25
    Tool 6—Beat The Clock (Grades 1-8/Ages 6-13) 26
    Tool 7—Do-Nothing Chair (Grades K-5/Ages 5-10) 27
    Tool 8—My Special Time (Grades K-8/Ages 5-13) 28
    Tool 9—Bus Rides (Grades K-3/Ages 5-8) 29
    Tool 10—Where Are The Limits? (Grades 4-12/Ages 9-18) 30
    Tool 11—Opportunity Time (Grades K-8/Ages 5-13) 32
    Tool 12—Responding (Adults) 33
    Tool 13—Encouragement Tips (Adults) 34

TOOLS FOR GETTING ACQUAINTED 35

    Tool 14—Name Tag (Grades 1-Adult/Ages 6 and up) 37
    Tool 15—Whose Shoes? (Grades 5-Adult/Ages 10 and up) 38
    Tool 16—Interview (Grades K-8/Ages 5-13) 39
    Tool 17—Getting To Know You (Grades 4-Adult/Ages 9 and up) 40
    Tool 18—Name Card (Grades 4-Adult/Ages 9 and up) 41
    Tool 19—Search For Someone (Grades 3-Adult/Ages 8 and up) 42
    Tool 20—Name Game (Grades 2-Adult/Ages 7 and up) 44
    Tool 21—People Tree (Grades 1-Adult/Ages 6 and up) 45
    Tool 22—"Hot Seat" Interview (Grades 3-12/Ages 8-18) 46
    Tool 23—Open-Ended Sentences (Grades 4-12/Ages 9-18) 47
    Tool 24—Reminiscing (Grades 4-12/Ages 9-18) 48
    Tool 25—Fantasy (Grades 4-12/Ages 9-18) 49
    Tool 26—Positive Participation (Grades 5-12/Ages 10-18) 50

Tool 27—Scavenger Hunt (Grades 6-12/Ages 11-18) 51

Tool 28—Get-Acquainted Bingo (Grades 6-12/Ages 11-18) 52

Tool 29—Toilet Paper (Grades 7-Adult/Ages 12 and up) 54

TOOLS FOR ENCOURAGING FEELINGS COMMUNICATION 55

Tool 30—My Word (Grades 1-8/Ages 6-13) 57

Tool 31—Finding Feelings (Grades K-8/Ages 5-13) 58

Tool 32—Feeling Stories (Grades 3-12/Ages 8-18) 59

Tool 33—Masks Of Feelings (Grades 3-8/Ages 8-13) 60

Tool 34—Feeling Cards (Grades 2-8/Ages 7-13) 61

Tool 35—Imaginary Box (Grades 3-Adult/Ages 8 and up) 62

Tool 36—Maintaining My Package (Grades 4-Adult/Ages 9 and up) 63

Tool 37—Learning To Listen (Grades 4-12/Ages 9-18) 64

Tool 38—One Word Communication (Grades 4-Adult/Ages 9 and up) 66

TOOLS FOR BUILDING SELF ESTEEM 67

Tool 39—Significant Strokes (Grades 4-Adult/Ages 9 and up) 69

Tool 40—All About Me (Grades 2-5/Ages 7-10) 70

Tool 41—My Most Exciting Adventure (Grades K-Adult/Ages 5 and up) 71

Tool 42—My Success Record (Grades 1-8/Ages 6-13) 72

Tool 43—My Success Chart (Grades 3-12/Ages 8-18) 73

Tool 44—Sweet To My Ear (Grades 4-12/Ages 9-18) 74

Tool 45—Mirror, Mirror On The Wall (Grades 3-8/Ages 8-13) 75

Tool 46—Design A T-Shirt (Grades 4-Adult/Ages 9 and up) 76

Tool 47—I Betcha Didn't Know (Grades 3-Adult/Ages 8 and up) 77

Tool 48—Secret Encouragement (Grades 4-Adult/Ages 9 and up) 78

Tool 49—Card File (Grades 4-12/Ages 9-18) 79

Tool 50—Birthday Candles (Grades 4-8/Ages 9-13) 80

Tool 51—Spotlighting (Grades 4-Adult/Ages 9 and up) 81

Tool 52—I Am (Grades 6-Adult/Ages 11 and up) 82

Tool 53—My Well (Grades 2-5/Ages 7-10) 84

TOOLS FOR FINDING SOLUTIONS 85

Tool 54—Brainstorming (Grades 4-Adult/Ages 9 and up) 87

Tool 55—Goal Setting (Grades 4-12/Ages 9-18) 88

Tool 56—Listening Vocabulary (Grades 2-12/Ages 7-18) 90

Tool 57—Decision Making (Grades 4-12/Ages 9-18) 91

Tool 58—Six Steps To Problem Solving (Grades 5-Adult/Ages 10 and up) 92

Tool 59—Problem-Solving Exercise (Grades 5-12/Ages 10-18) 94

Tool 60—Team Building (Grades 4-Adult/Ages 9 and up) 95

Tool 61—Conflict Resolution (Grades 5-Adult/Ages 10 and up) 96

Tool 62—Team Building Roles (Grades 9-Adult/Ages 14 and up) 98

Tool 63—Jumping Hurdles (Grades 4-12/Ages 9-18) 100

Tool 64—Attitudes Toward Authority (Adults) 101
Tool 65—Role-Play (Grades 2-Adult/Ages 7 and up) 104

TOOLS FOR DEEPENING UNDERSTANDING 105

Tool 66—Open-Ended Sentences (Grades 1-12/Ages 6-18) 107
Tool 67—Friendship (Grades 4-Adult/Ages 9 and up) 108
Tool 68—Promote Friendship (Grades K-8/Ages 5-13) 109
Tool 69—Friendship Banner (Grades 4-8/Ages 9-13) 110
Tool 70—Water Fantasy (Grades 4-Adult/Ages 9 and up) 111
Tool 71—Opinion (Grades 9-Adult/Ages 14 and up) 112
Tool 72—A Gestalt Activity (Grades 4-Adult/Ages 9 and up) 113
Tool 73—Projection (Grades 3-Adult/Ages 8 and up) 114
Tool 74—Looking Back (Grades 5-Adult/Ages 10 and up) 115
Tool 75—Inside/Outside (Grades 4-Adult/Ages 9 and up) 116
Tool 76—Myself/Yourself (Grades K-4/Ages 5-9) 117
Tool 77—Share A Quote (Grades 6-Adult/Ages 11 and up) 118
Tool 78—Learning Check Up (Grades 4-12/Ages 9-18) 119
Tool 79—Household (Grades 5-Adult/Ages 10 and up) 120
Tool 80—Individuality Cookie (Grades 2-Adult/Ages 7 and up) 121
Tool 81—Open-Ended Exchange (Grades 4-Adult/Ages 9 and up) 122
Tool 82—Turning Points (Grades 5-Adult/Ages 10 and up) 124
Tool 83—Likenesses and Differences (Grades 4-12/Ages 9-18) 125
Tool 84—Prejudice (Grades 4-12/Ages 9-18) 126
Tool 85—Cooperative Poster (Grades 6-Adult/Ages 11 and up) 127
Tool 86—Values Pie (Grades 6-Adult/Ages 11 and up) 128
Tool 87—Journal Keeping (Grades 4-Adult/Ages 9 and up) 129
Tool 88—Little Things About Me (Grades 6-Adult/Ages 11 and up) 130
Tool 89—All About Me (Grades 5-12/Ages 10-18) 131
Tool 90—My Social Self (Grades 4-Adult/Ages 9 and up) 134
Tool 91—Group Communication (Grades 4-Adult/Ages 9 and up) 136
Tool 92—What If? (Grades 4-12/Ages 9-18) 138
Tool 93—Miracles (Grades 4-Adult/Ages 9 and up) 140
Tool 94—Rank Order (Grades 6-12/Ages 11-18) 142
Tool 95—Personal Time Capsules (Grades 4-10/Ages 9-16) 144
Tool 96—Profile (Grades 6-Adult/Ages 11 and up) 146
Tool 97—Family (Grades 4-12/Ages 9-18) 148

TOOLS FOR CAREER AWARENESS 149

Tool 98—What Do You Want To Do? (Grades 6-12/Ages 11-18) 151
Tool 99—Career Consequences Cards (Grades 3-8/Ages 8-13) 152
Tool 100—People Who Work In Our School (Grades 3-5/Ages 8-10) 154
Tool 101—Your Resume (Grades 6-12/Ages 11-18) 156
Tool 102—Journalist (Grades 3-Adult/Ages 8 and up) 157

EVALUATION 158
ABOUT THE AUTHOR 160

INTRODUCTION

The material in this book has been created and collected over a period of twenty years working with groups. Some of the activities are my own, created from a need apparent in the group. Some are expanded ideas based on an original concept which I have experienced. Some are old classics which have been with us for years and some of them are simply ideas to aid in group management.

My recognition and appreciation that these ideas belong to many people is very clear. They have landed in my files from conferences, workshops, handouts, and counselor sharings with long lost possibilities of identifying the original source.

These activities are varied in age level, focus, and objective. Although they are appropriate for churches, scouting groups, camps, retreats, and workshops, they are primarily designed for school counselors to use as classroom techniques or with small-group programs. Most of them can be appropriated by teachers or other leadership personnel for use in conferences or in the classroom.

—*Mary Joe Hannaford*

TO THE LEADER

What Is A Group?

Group counseling is an interpersonal process in which individuals with similar concerns explore with each other and a leader their feelings and attitudes about themselves or situations. Through their interpersonal relationships, each individual will discover alternative modes of thinking and behaving. Participants learn to help others as well as obtaining help for themselves.

Why Have A Group?

A group provides a safe, understanding, caring, participating, and approving environment. It is a place where participants can be open and honest, test their ideas and solutions, and obtain frank evaluations of their efforts to change.

A group is useful for several reasons:

1. The leader has an opportunity to know the participants more intimately.

2. Participants build a support group with each other which can continue outside the group setting.

3. A specific time is set for the development of this relationship.

4. Participants build confidence and self-esteem.

5. Participants begin to see that other people have needs and problems similar to their own.

How To Organize A Group

Groups can be organized by:

1. Getting teachers or parents to recommend participants who have specific needs.

2. Sending out a flyer or placing an announcement on the bulletin board and having participants volunteer to participate.

3. Selecting participants whom you have seen individually and inviting them to participate.

Church or organizational groups can be formed by simply announcing the formation of the group and its purpose, followed by letting people sign up.

What To Do In A Group

1. Structure the group so that you accomplish your purpose.

2. Use exercises that stimulate group discussion.

3. Begin with an icebreaker to enhance group relationships.

4. Set appropriate lengths of time for the group according to age level and situation. Thirty minutes is usually long enough for a young group while forty-five to fifty minutes to two hours can be appropriated for more mature participants. Situations such as school settings accommodate well to the forty-five to fifty minute class period.

5. Meet one time or for a series of six to eight weeks, depending on your goals for the group. Once a week for eight weeks seems to give time for some goal achievement. Some groups used principally for support may continue indefinitely. Have the participants complete an *Evaluation* (page 158) at the completion of the group experience or at an appropriate time during the group experience.

HINTS TO FOLLOW

Working with groups can be a challenging and rewarding experience if good techniques are learned and used. The following suggestions may be helpful in managing a group.

1. Keep on the subject and encourage full participation from the group, but assure each member of the right to say, "I pass." Participants will want to remain in a group that maintains an acceptable comfort level.

2. Use the activities in this book as educational experiences rather than therapeutic ones. No effort has been made to deepen the group into experiences which will stir too much emotion.

3. Be aware of maintaining a relaxed attitude and enthusiasm toward the ideas which are being presented. The body language and voice tone of the leader will largely determine the comfort level of the members of the group.

4. Clarify the basic principles being explored so that they are easily applied to specific needs of group members. Make these principles easy to discuss and simple to understand.

5. Avoid making definite statements or answering questions in such a way that members are robbed of being their own problem solvers.

6. Admit your own weaknesses and limitation of knowledge. Demonstrate the "courage to be imperfect."

As the leader, you may find the following phrases helpful in responding to the discussions held in the group setting.

- That's an interesting point, how do the rest of you feel about this?

- You may be right about that.

- Does anyone else have an idea?

- Can anyone think of an example which may apply to what has been mentioned?

- Why do you think that is so difficult to do?

- I wonder if anyone else has had a similar experience?

- Let's think about that.

- What do you think—what would you say about that?

- How do you feel about this point?

- It seems to me that we are rambling.

- Let's get back to the point.

- Does anyone have a different interpretation for that?

- You seem puzzled about that—tell us what you are thinking.

- Do we agree on that idea or does this idea bother any of you?

- What suggestions does the group have?

- How else could this problem be handled?

- Has anyone else tried this approach?

- Would you be willing to tell us about it?

- Have you read or discussed anything before that would apply here?

GROUP STRUCTURES

Varying the methods of group sharing can be very effective. Study the following structures for ideas which may work successfully with various groups. Consider your comfort level, the group comfort level, and the size of your group.

Dyads, Triads

Some exercises work well if shared between only two people in the group (dyads). The participants may share with the partner, then reverse the roles. This one-to-one relationship can be much less threatening than speaking or acting in a larger group. It is a good technique to use in the beginning stages when group comfort has not been established. With three people (triads) the same concept can be used or one person can participate at a time while another is listener and the third the observer. The observer can then report back to the whole group concerning the process and conclusions made in that triad. An additional advantage of using two or three people is the time saved by not having to wait for each participant to share in a larger group. The obvious disadvantage to dyads and triads is that the participants become involved with very few people and have minimal direct monitoring by the leader. Reporting back to the entire group can also be difficult if the entire group is very large.

Small Groups

Many activities work best in groups of six to eight. This arrangement enables each person to participate and receive responses from the group. Be sure these people sit in a circle or arrangement where they can see each other.

Fishbowl (Inner and Outer Circles)

This structure is effective in teaching listening and responding skills. The inner circle (half the group) is given a sentence completion or discussion topic to talk about. The other half, in the outer circle, listens without commenting, watching the group process in the inner circle. They then switch positions so that the new inner circle can participate.

Buzz Groups

One question or a series of related questions are assigned for discussion to several small, informal groups. At the end of the discussion period, these groups report back to the general group. This draws all members into the discussion involving them in the problem and the solution.

Role-Playing

Participants spontaneously act out problems in human relations. The enactment is then analyzed by both the observers and the role-players.

These basic principles should be followed in role-playing:

a. **Define the group problem**—group wants or needs.

b. **Establish a situation**—the situation must provide enough content to make it seem real and to give the players and observers a common orientation.

c. **Cast the characters**—it is important to choose persons who can carry out that role well and who will not be threatened or exposed by it. Start beginners in roles in which they feel at home and confident.

d. **Produce the performance**—set some structure but generally let the characters be free to develop spontaneously. Stop the role-play when there is enough information for the group to process, when the players reach an impasse, or when there is a natural closing.

e. **Discuss and analyze the situation and the behavior**—relate the role-play to the original problem. Focus on the contribution to the problem solving. Avoid commenting on the acting ability of the players. Identify what has been learned.

Brainstorming

Brainstorming is a rapid-fire session where all members state all ideas which come to mind on a specified topic. No attempt is made to evaluate at this time. A recorder writes down all the ideas mentioned. This method is especially helpful in generating ideas for further discussion, introducing a topic, or leading into a planning project. The brainstorming session is followed by careful analysis and evaluation of these ideas. Further information can be found on page 87.

TOOLS
FOR

STARTING
GROUPS

GROUP STARTERS
(Grades K-Adult/Ages 5 and up)

Objective:

To provide the leader with some quick, non-threatening activities which will break the tension of starting a new group

Materials:

None.

Procedure:

Although many of the activities included in this book can be used as group starters, sometimes it is convenient to have a few activities on hand which are very non-threatening and provide just plain fun. Try some of the following activities:

Favorites:

Ask each person to choose a favorite—activity, food, place, TV show, movie, book, etc. When each person has shared his/her favorite with the group, see who can remember the most about the other participants.

Simon Says:

This is an old game which is always fun. The leader says, "Simon says, Hold up your left arm—Simon says, Turn your left thumb down." If Simon doesn't say it and the group members respond, they have to sit out the remainder of the game. The last persons still in the game are the winners.

Description:

Simply ask for three adjectives to describe any activity which is current. For example: school, games, current events, etc.

Humor:

Tell about the funniest thing that has happened to you in the last week.

Left Person:

Give the name and a descriptive word about the person on your left. Allow time for this exchange of names. Let this be accumulative as they go around the room, repeating all the names mentioned by the group members who proceeded them.

Clothespin:

Give each person three or four clothespins. Begin with one group member telling something about him/herself. If any other person has had a similar experience he/she pins a clothespin on the storyteller. This encourages listening and empathy. Repeat this process with the other group members.

Group Picture:

Using a large piece of drawing paper and a magic marker, draw a simple picture or a line. Then pass the materials around the group and ask each person to add something simple to the picture. At the end, ask for an interpretation of the picture and discuss the feeling of cooperation.

Free Association:

The leader says a word and points to a person in the group. That person says the first word that comes to mind when stimulated by the word said. Then the leader repeats the word and points to another person, continuing the process until several participants have responded. The leader continues the activity using different words.

Descriptive Adjective:

Have the participants introduce themselves with an adjective that begins with the same letter as their first name—Beautiful Betty, Marvelous Mary, Proud Peter, Crazy Chris. Let these accumulate so that the last person is saying all the names and adjectives.

Travel:

Start around the circle with "I am going on a trip and I am going to take." Each item added must be named alphabetically. "I am going on a trip and I am going to take an **A**pple." "I am going on a trip and I am going to take a **B**ear." "I am going on a trip and I am going to take a **C**ar." This is cumulative. All persons must say all the words that have been given before them. For example: "I am going on a trip and I am going to take an **A**pple, a **B**ear, a **C**ar—then he/she adds his/her own item.

Aladdin's Lamp:

You may tell the story of Aladdin if the group doesn't know it. When you have finished the story, tell the group they are each going to be given three wishes. Give each person time to express his/her wishes. This exercise can also be done without the story.

DISCUSSION STARTERS

(Grades 4-Adult/Ages 9 and up)

Objective:

To provide the leader with good questions which stimulate discussion and lead participants to a deeper level of communication

Materials:

☐ List of questions (see below)

Procedure:

A good question can often be the best way of getting a group or class stimulated into thinking philosophically. It can also encourage an atmosphere of freedom to express opinions.

The basic rules must be:

- Everyone who wishes one gets a turn.
- There will be no judgments made.
- There will be no "put-downs."

Some ideas for questions are:

What is self-awareness? _____

What is subconscious? _____

What is responsibility? _____

What is a profession? _____

What is life? _____

What is influence? _____

What is a leader?_____

What is reality? _____

What is creativity? _____

What is peace? _____

What is stress? _____

How have the following influenced me and how have I influenced them?

My birth date, my age _____

My height, my weight _____

My physical characteristics _____

My intelligence, abilities, talents _____

My job, my career _____

My education _____

My appearance _____

My social communication _____

My parents' attitudes _____

My personal attitudes _____

My sex _____

My values _____

My thoughts _____

My feelings _____

My happiness _____

My friends _____

My fun _____

My popularity _____

My fears, anxieties _____

My love relationships _____

Give the participants time to respond to the questions/influences with descriptive answers. Identify the level of control each of us has over each item and how our personal choices and responsibility affect outcomes. Add to this list any questions or influences which seem appropriate.

TOOLS FOR

GROUP OR CLASSROOM MANAGEMENT

HELP

(Grades K-4/Ages 5-9)

Objective:

To provide an orderly method of responding to student requests for assistance

Materials:

- [ ] Signs reading *HELP,* popsicle sticks, and box

or

- [ ] Table with a *HELP* sign
- [ ] Numbered tickets such as those used in a delicatessen (optional)

Procedure:

Every large-group leader sometimes faces the frustration of having many hands raised or a number of children calling for help at the same time. One effective way to handle this distraction follows.

Prepare *HELP* signs on popsicle sticks for students who need assistance from the leader. This will prevent crowding around the leader or teacher's desk, frequent tugs on the sleeve, or hands waving wildly in the air. Keep the *HELP* signs in a box. When children need help, they will quietly get a sign from the box and hold it in their hands until the teacher/leader gets there.

Alternatives:

Have a *HELP* table. When children need help, they move quietly to the table and wait for their turn with the leader/teacher. Set a limit for the number of children that can be at the table at one time.

Have the children take numbers such as those used in a delicatessen. The child may hold up his/her number or go to the table in the appropriate order to wait for help.

FOOTSTEPS
(Grades K-4/Ages 5-9)

Objective:

To teach participants cooperation through a group activity

Materials:

☐ 8 pieces of paper large enough for footprints and 4 markers for each group

Procedure:

Have the group members discuss a destination or a place where they would like to go in the near vicinity. Divide the class into groups of four. Distribute eight pieces of paper and four markers to each group. Have the children trace each others' footprints on the paper. When the groups come back together, have one group leader from each foursome lay its papers end-to-end to make a long footpath which will end at the destination which they have chosen. Give time for each group member to walk down the pathway to the destination. When the activity is completed, discuss with the children what they saw happening as they worked together.

Use the following questions to promote discussion.

- How did you decide to work together?

- Was it important to work together or could you have done this exercise alone?

- Was the goal accomplished?

- Where did you see areas of disagreement? agreement?

- What is the meaning of *cooperation*?

- Can a task be accomplished more satisfactorily when there is cooperation?

- Using cooperation, did each person get to the destination?

You may want to help the children relate this activity to things which need to be accomplished in school, at home, or in the community such as playing a team sport, arranging the room, accomplishing an academic task, completing chores, picking up trash in a neighborhood, or cleaning a streambed.

GRUMPY PILLOW

(Grades K-4/Ages 5-9)

Objective:

To give participants permission to be angry by providing a healthy outlet for their behavior

Materials:

☐ A pillow labeled "Grumpy Pillow"

Procedure:

When children are angry about something or feel grumpy, they may need to talk about their feelings. One way to handle this when an adult is not available for the child to talk with is to use to an inanimate object such as a pillow. Children will soon learn the location of the "Grumpy Pillow" and know they can say anything they want to the pillow. If they are intensely angry, they may need permission to hit the pillow or to throw it in an appropriate way. Using a bean bag for this purpose is also effective.

Teach children to throw the pillow at a wall outside to dissolve anger and to learn safe ways of getting rid of irritation. Children must be told what the limitations are so that they do not hurt others, themselves, animals, or property when they are angry. It is very important that they understand that it is often all right to be angry. It must be clear that it is the behavior that accompanies the anger that must be safe.

BEAT THE CLOCK

(Grades 1-8/Ages 6-13)

Objective:

To motivate children to complete tasks on time

Materials:

☐ A calendar or a form as shown below

Procedure:

Some children seem to have difficulty completing assigned tasks. Give the "lagging" child one of the forms below or use a regular calendar. Have the child specify the subject or task which seems difficult for him/her complete. Some examples might be: read 10 pages of a library book each day, complete all math class work, work on science report, make the bed, put dirty clothes in the hamper. The student will check the box each day his/her work is completed by the time specified by the leader. If he/she has a check in the *Completed* box every day for one week, a trade can be made for 10 minutes of free time or whatever reward seems appropriate.

Warning! Be sure children have a reachable goal, so that they can experience some success. If the task is too difficult, they will become discouraged and quit before trying.

NAME _____

☆ TASK TO BE COMPLETED THIS WEEK ☆

[   ]

MONDAY	☐ Completed	☐ Not Completed
TUESDAY	☐ Completed	☐ Not Completed
WEDNESDAY	☐ Completed	☐ Not Completed
THURSDAY	☐ Completed	☐ Not Completed
FRIDAY	☐ Completed	☐ Not Completed

DO-NOTHING CHAIR
(Grades K-5/Ages 5-10)

Objective:

To promote decision-making for the student who is uncooperative in completing work in class (This exercise uses a theory called paradoxical intention to encourage participation in the work required.)

Materials:

☐ A chair in a secluded area of the room

Procedure:

Some students respond well to the opportunity to choose "not to work." This technique allows students the privilege to *choose* to work. Prepare a chair or an area where they are allowed to "just sit." This time will often become monotonous and boring, provide a refreshing rest, or will motivate production by choice rather than nagging, thus upgrading the quality of students' work. For example, the leader might say:

> "John, I have noticed that during the past week, you have been uninterested in doing the assignments. Since you have decided that you do not want to participate, I have arranged a special chair where you can do nothing if you want to. You will just sit here and there will be no assignments. When you decide that you want to cooperate with the class, you can come and tell me, and we will work out a way for you to catch up."

This must be stated in a soft understanding voice communicating a real sense of permission to do nothing.

Warning! Rules regarding conduct in the no-work area must be clearly understood. If the student's withdrawal continues over a week, other measures, such as referral to the school counselor, should be initiated. Students may be re-entered gradually back to the academic area. They may come back to reading and math, but not other subjects until they are able to fit in and cooperate.

An understanding with the parents of what you are trying to accomplish with this method will protect public relations.

MY SPECIAL TIME

(Grades K-8/Ages 5-13)

Objective:

To supply children the need for attention without disruption to the regular schedule

Materials:

☐ Sign up sheet for appointments and copies of *We Have An Appointment* (see below)

Procedure:

Some students often seem to be in constant need of attention. Teachers will find them at their desks or beside them every few minutes. One way to handle this need for attention is not to deny it, but to satisfy it. Tell the students that you are anxious to have some time together with them. Make an appointment for a 10-minute session at a time of the day between assignments or while other students are busy with desk work. Write the appointment on a *We Have An Appointment* sheet in the presence of the student so that he/she will know that it is definite. If they "hang around" before the appointment, have them be seated with a reminder that you have a special time set for them at _____(announce the time).

Alternative:

A sign up sheet can be posted on a bulletin board specifying the times the teacher will be available for individual appointments. Students can sign up for a 10-minute conference or a special time to talk individually.

STUDENT'S NAME

~WE HAVE AN APPOINTMENT~

☞ on _____ at ____:____

SIGNATURE

BUS RIDES

(Grades K-3/Ages 5-8)

Objective:

To assist students in boarding the correct bus (This is a good activity for the opening weeks of school.)

Materials:

☐ Bulletin board, yellow construction paper, and marker

Procedure:

At the opening of school, it may be especially hard for the students to remember their bus numbers. Cut out yellow construction paper in the shape of school busses about three inches long. Write each student's name and bus number on a bus and post them on a bulletin board in alphabetical order. Explain the board to the students on the first day of school. Remind them to report any bus changes. This will also help teachers to find students' busses quickly.

WHERE ARE THE LIMITS?
(Grades 4-12/Ages 9-18)

Objective:

To enhance students' quality of work by seeing that they are clearly informed about rules and limits

Materials:

☐ Flipchart and marker or chalkboard and chalk
☐ Copy of *Limits and Freedom* (page 31) and pencil for each participant

Procedure:

Students work best when they are clearly informed about rules and limits. However, within those limits are areas where they also should have the freedom to make their own decisions and initiate their own plans. Many problems can be avoided if these limits and freedoms are clearly stated ahead of time and reviewed when necessary to clarify their understanding.

Distribute a copy of *Limits and Freedom* and a pencil to each student. Ask them to write the limits or rules in each category which govern their behaviors. List the group members answers for each category in the appropriate area on the chalkboard or flipchart. Examples might include:

- Hang up your coat in the closet before coming to your seat.
- All homework will be due upon entering the room.
- Bedtime for children is at 10:00 P.M.
- No play time until homework is completed.

In the center rectangle, have the students write things which they are free to decide, explaining that this is their area of freedom. Examples might include:

- You may choose the games you play at play period.
- You may choose your partner for study time.
- You may choose your food at lunch.
- You may spend your allowance as you like.

It is essential for students to understand that all people have limitations beyond which they cannot go without serious consequences. Clarify this concept by discussing the following:

- Why is it important to have limits?
- What do we learn from having limits?
- What happens when we do not understand or keep the limits?
- Why is it important to have some freedoms?
- What do we learn from having freedoms?
- What happens when we do not respect our freedoms or misuse them?

LIMITS AND FREEDOM

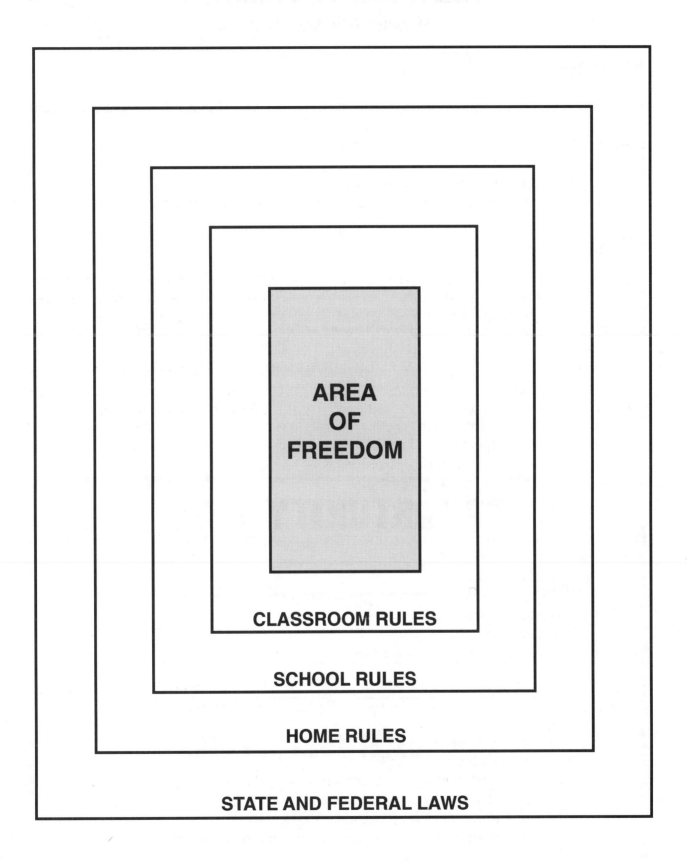

AREA
OF
FREEDOM

CLASSROOM RULES

SCHOOL RULES

HOME RULES

STATE AND FEDERAL LAWS

OPPORTUNITY TIME

(Grades K-8/Ages 5-13)

Objective:

To reward good work with a visit to an adult in the school who is in a prestigious position (For example: principal, custodian, special teacher, secretary, etc.)

Materials:

☐ Copies of *Opportunity Time* (see below)

Procedure:

Reward students' good work or behavior by arranging a positive appointment with an adult chosen by the student in the school. Arrange a time with the chosen adult and ask him/her to spend 10-15 minutes talking with the student or group of students, playing a table game, or allowing them to help, in order to develop a friendly atmosphere of reinforcement. The adult chosen may be prepared to share an article in a magazine, a picture of his/her family, show something he/she uses for the job, or play a short game.

A report back to the class may encourage other students to work for the same privilege. (This activity also gives the adult an opportunity to know students in a positive way.)

OPPORTUNITY TIME

Student's name _____

Let's get together on _____

From_____

To _____

✳ FOR SOMETHING SPECIAL ✳

See you then,

_____

RESPONDING

(Adults)

Objective:

To present ways the counselor or teacher can respond to participants, parents, or other teachers appropriately to encourage communication

Materials:

☐ Any reminders needed of the following possibilities

Procedure:

Responses are most effective when you:

1. Make and use rules so the limits are clear.

2. Use one of the following statements:

   • What can we do that would bring a result for your best interest?
   • What kind of contract can we make with each other? (Include task and time)

3. State your own need in the form of an "I" message. Then give recipients a chance to state their needs.

4. Stay out of a power struggle!

   • Capitalize on your skills; listening and confronting.
   • Encourage worthwhile actions and attitudes.
   • Discuss actions privately.
   • Employ role-playing.
   • Respect feelings.
   • Give permission to own the feelings.
   • Avoid getting "hooked."

5. Listen

   • Use attending behavior.
   • Use responding behavior.

6. Remember reflecting skills

   • "You feel ."
   • "You feel that   ."
   • "You feel that _____ because ."

ENCOURAGEMENT TIPS
(Adults)

Objective:

To present examples of statements which encourage and examples of statements which discourage

Materials:

☐ Copies of *Encouraging Statements/Discouraging Statements* (see below) for teachers, parents or other persons working with participants

Procedure:

Distribute a copy of the statements to each participant. Read the statements aloud and see if the group agrees with their placement in the categories of *Encouraging Statements* or *Discouraging Statements.* Discuss the reasons for the participants agreement or disagreement. Remember voice tone and body language will highly influence the way the statement is perceived.

ENCOURAGING STATEMENTS:

- I am glad you enjoyed doing that.
- That made you feel really proud.
- You have made progress since the last marking period.
- I like the way you stuck to that project.
- We all make mistakes sometimes.
- Your listening has really improved.
- I believe you can do it. If you have any trouble, let me know, and I'll be glad to help.
- Let's think it through together.
- I really admire the way you are trying.
- You have really improved.
- I'm glad you keep trying even though it is tough sometimes.

DISCOURAGING STATEMENTS:

- Be careful—you might fall and hurt yourself.
- You're just lazy and won't ever pay attention.
- Why didn't you think of that before you started.
- You're old enough to know better than that.
- Let me help you, you might break it.
- If you keep that up, you'll never amount to anything.
- Don't forget your coat!
- I'm glad you turned your paper in on time, but it should have been neater.
- It would be great if you could read as well as your sister.

TOOLS
FOR

GETTING
ACQUAINTED

NAME TAG

(Grades 1-Adult/Ages 6 and up)

Objective:

To help participants learn each other's names and to present an opportunity to get acquainted

Materials:

- ☐ Construction paper in a variety of colors, pieces of yarn long enough to hang around the neck, crayons or magic markers, and scissors for each participant
- ☐ Holepunch

Procedure:

Place different-colored construction paper, yarn, scissors, and crayons or markers on a table.

Tell the participants to create a name tag by choosing a color of construction paper, then cutting the paper into a shape that is representative of their personalities. When the participants have finished, they should write their names on the paper with the marker, large enough to be easily seen. Punch two holes in the top of each nametag and string a piece of yarn through both holes. Have the participants hang their nametags around their necks so that their names can be easily seen.

Note: A variation could be to shape the paper like a state, the school, or other readily identifiable forms.

Have the participants form groups of four members. Tell them that each group member will have one minute to introduce him/herself and explain the reasons for the color and shape of his/her nametag to the other group members. At the end of four minutes, call time and have the participants form new groups. Repeat the process until everyone has met everyone else or the allotted time has elapsed.

WHOSE SHOES?

(Grades 5-Adult/Ages 10 and up)

Objective:

To increase the participants' power of observation and to help them get to know each other better

Materials:

☐ Sheet of paper and a pencil for each participant

Procedure:

Note: This activity will necessitate name tags or some assurance that all the group members know each other's names.

Distribute a piece of paper and a pencil to each participant. Have the participants form groups of an appropriate size for their age levels—smaller groups for younger children, larger groups for older children/adults. Ask each person to take off both shoes and place them in the middle of the group. Mix the shoes up. Then say, "We are going to follow an old Japanese custom of removing the shoes when entering a house. Number your paper according to the number of people in our group." Hold up one pair of shoes at a time and have the group members write down the name of the owner. When they have finished writing, hold up each pair of shoes and let the owner claim them as the participants check their answers.

INTERVIEW

(Grades K-8/Ages 5-13)

Objective:

To assist participants in getting acquainted and developing self-confidence and poise

Materials:

☐ Cassette recorder, audio tape (optional)

Procedure:

The leader and the group members should sit in a circle. Be sure that the participants can see each other. The leader begins by asking questions of the child on his/her left. Choose an appropriate number of questions for the age level of your group. After the child has a chance to answer, that child turns to the child on his/her left and follows the same procedure. This continues until each group member has had a turn being interviewed. Then ask the participants to share what they have learned about each other, things that they have in common, and ways they are different.

Questions that are appropriate are:

- What is your name?
- What is your favorite color?
- What do you like the most (least) about school?
- What do you like to do on Saturdays?
- What pets do you have?
- Where were you born?
- Where did you grow up?
- How many children are in your family?
- What is your favorite food?
- Who is your favorite movie star?
- Who is your favorite TV star?
- Who is your favorite athlete?
- What is your favorite book?

If you choose to do so, record the whole interview on the tape recorder. When the interviews are complete, play them back. This can be done before the participants share their answers to give them a second chance to learn more, or after they have shared their answers to check the correctness of their responses.

GETTING TO KNOW YOU

(Grades 4-Adult/Ages 9 and up)

Objective:

To encourage the group members to get acquainted

Materials:

☐ Four statements (see below) written on a chalkboard or flipchart

Procedure:

Instruct the group members to shake hands and introduce themselves by name to four people. When this is completed, inform the participants that the last person they introduced themselves to will be their partner. Display on the chalkboard/flipchart the following statements:

1. The newest thing I own is…

2. The last place I visited was…

3. The last book I read was…

4. Something most people don't know about me is…

Then tell the partners to share with each other the answers to the statements written on the chalkboard/flipchart. When this is completed, have each couple pair up with another couple and share what they have learned about their partners. Then have the groups of four exchange partners within their group. The new couples should then pair up with a new couple and repeat the activity. Continue having the couples pair up with other couples, exchange partners, and pair up with new couples for as long as time allows.

NAME CARD
(Grades 4-Adult/Ages 9 and up)

Objective:

To assist the group members in establishing relationships

To structure an opportunity for participants to learn the name of and some facts about each person

Materials:

☐ 7" x 9" card, marker, pencil, and pins for each participant
☐ Made-up sample card (see below)

Procedure:

Distribute a 7" x 9" card, marker, and pencil to each participant. Tell the participants to write their first names in large letters in the center of the card with markers. Then say:

> "After you have your written name in the center of the card, mark off each corner with two inch squares. (Show the sample card.) Place one of the following titles at the top of each square: *Decision, Favorites, People,* and *Places.* Now fill in the squares with the answers to these statements."

Read the following statements aloud and give the participants time to fill in their cards a word or two.

- Write the most recent decision you had to make.
- Write your favorite food and color.
- Write the name of the person you admire most.
- Write the name of a place you would like to travel to.

When all the squares are complete, divide the participants into groups of four and ask them to share one of their squares with the other members. If time permits, rotate the groups and have them choose another square. If the group is small, this can be done with the whole group. When sharing is completed, have the members pin the cards on their shirts so that their names are easily visible.

This is a good-kick off activity for discussions on values or conflicts.

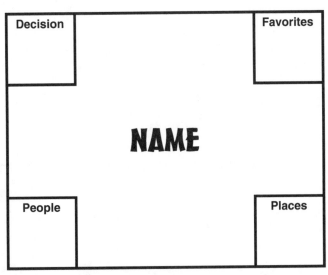

SEARCH FOR SOMEONE

(Grades 3-Adult/Ages 8 and up)

Objective:

To provide a way for participants to get acquainted in a group or class if they do not know each other or have been separated over the summer months

Materials:

☐ Copy of *Search Triangle* (page 43) and a pencil for each participant

Procedure:

Distribute a copy of *Search Triangle* and a pencil to each participant. Tell them to read the instructions at the bottom of the page and have other group members fill in the spaces by signing or initialing the appropriate squares. (Only one signature is allowed per person.) When the task is completed, allow time for the participants to share their findings.

SEARCH TRIANGLE

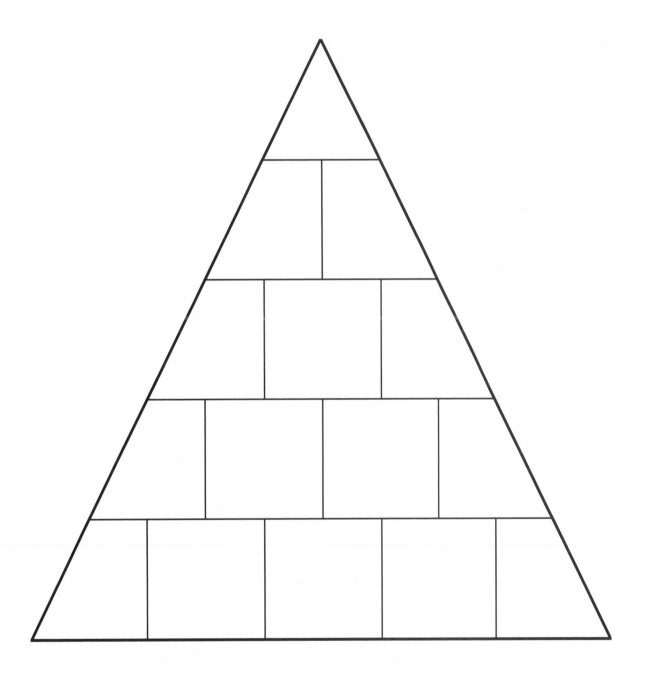

FIND:

1 PERSON WHO CROSSED A BODY OF WATER THIS SUMMER.
2 PEOPLE WHO WENT ON A TRIP DURING THE SUMMER.
3 PEOPLE WHO MADE SOMETHING THIS SUMMER.
4 PEOPLE WHO HAVE READ A BOOK FOR FUN DURING THE PAST MONTH.
5 PEOPLE WHO HAVE BEEN IN THIS SCHOOL FOR AT LEAST 3 YEARS.

NAME GAME

(Grades 2-Adult/Ages 7 and up)

Objective:

To help group members learn names and establish positive feelings toward themselves and their fellow group members

Materials:

None.

Procedure:

Have the group sit or stand in a circle. The leader sets the tone by starting in the following manner.

"My name is Nancy Wright."

The second person says,

"This is Nancy Wright and I am Sam Summers."

The third person says,

"This is Nancy Wright and Sam Summers and I am Susan Williams."

Continue around the circle until Nancy Wright says the name of each person in the circle.

Alternatives:

Use the same method as above except this time add an adjective to describe each person.

"My name is Exciting Nancy Wright."
"This is Exciting Nancy Wright and I am Silly Sam Summers."
"This is Exciting Nancy Wright, Silly Sam Summers, and I am Spontaneous Susan Williams."

Continue around the circle until you return to the leader.

Use the same format as above except this time the adjective must be a feeling word describing how the participant feels at the moment.

"My name is Happy Nancy."
"This is Happy Nancy, and I am Serious Sam."
"This is Happy Nancy, Serious Sam, and I am Tired Susan."

PEOPLE TREE

(Grades 1-Adult/Ages 6 and up)

Objective:

To assist participants in getting acquainted

Materials:

- [ ] Bulletin board and outline of a "people tree" made from brown construction paper
- [ ] Symbols of your choice and markers for each participant

Procedure:

In a prominent place, attach the "people tree" to the bulletin board. Write each participant's name on an apple, a heart, a leaf, a holiday ornament, or other symbol of your choice. Give each participant his/her symbol. Instruct the participants to write a fact or draw a picture that represents them on the symbol. When the participants are finished, attach the symbols to the "people tree." Keep the "people tree" posted several weeks in order for participants to have plenty of time to find others and learn the facts about them.

"HOT SEAT" INTERVIEW

(Grades 3-12/Ages 8-18)

Objective:

To get better acquainted and to gain poise in appearing before a group

Materials:

☐ Chair labelled "Hot Seat"
☐ Copy of the list of questions (see below)

Procedure:

Place the "Hot Seat" in the center of the group. Ask for a volunteer to take the "Hot Seat." Appoint one person to be the interviewer and give that person the list of questions. Tell the other members of the group that they will observe while the appointed person asks the questions. *Note:* Two people can share the "Hot Seat" by putting two chairs in the center of the group. This will lower the threat level. Some rules may be necessary in order to prevent questions about sensitive issues. The following are examples of questions:

- Where do you live?
- Where were you born?
- Who lives in your house?
- What kind of pets do you have?
- What is your hobby?
- What is your favorite sport to play or watch?
- What is your favorite fun activity?
- What do you like about school?
- What is your favorite color?
- Where would you like to travel?
- What are you looking forward to next year?
- What is your favorite place to go?
- Who is your favorite hero?
- What is your favorite book? Why?
- What is your favorite piece of clothing?

When all the questions have been asked, time may be allowed for additional questions from the group.

OPEN-ENDED SENTENCES

(Grades 4-12/Ages 9-18)

Objective:

To assist participants in self-understanding

To guide a creative writing exercise

To give the leader insight into the participants' thinking and behavior

Materials:

☐ Copy of the list of *Open-Ended Sentences* (see below) for each participant

Procedures:

Distribute a copy of the *Open-Ended Sentences* to each participant. These sentences may be used in many ways—as an ice-breaker for a group or for a class writing activity. The sentences may be given one at a time, one a day, or as a list for seatwork or homework. Small-group discussions of the participants' sentence endings can give them a chance to better know themselves and each other.

OPEN-ENDED SENTENCES:

1. I am _____ .

2. If I could do anything I wanted _____ .

3. When I grow up _____ .

4. I wish I had more time to _____ .

5. My feelings get hurt when _____ .

6. I get really mad when _____ .

7. I am really happy when _____ .

8. I am very sad when _____ .

9. I enjoy my family most when _____ .

10. What I like most about myself is _____ .

11. The things that are most important to me are _____ .

12. One thing I would like to change is _____ .

13. A real friend is _____ .

14. I learn most when _____ .

15. I am most excited when _____ .

REMINISCING

(Grades 4-12/Ages 9-18)

Objective:

To structure some get-acquainted communication which is non-threatening and provides an opportunity for the group to laugh together

Materials:

☐ Flipchart and marker or chalkboard and chalk

Procedure:

Write the open-ended sentences (see below) on the chalkboard/flipchart. Instruct the group members to move into dyads, triads, or foursomes and sit facing each other. Tell the participants to read the sentences one at a time and allow each group member to respond before going on to the next sentence. The leader may read the sentences aloud to the groups.

OPEN-ENDED SENTENCES:

1. The first time I tried to swim _____ .

2. The first time I tried to dance _____ .

3. The first time I went to school _____ .

4. The first time I tried to ice skate _____ .

5. The first time I cooked something _____ .

6. The first time I rode a bicycle _____ .

7. The first time I received a present _____ .

8. The first time I visited my grandparents _____ .

9. The first time I drove a car _____ .

10. The first time I flew in an airplane _____ .

11. The first time I got really sick _____ .

12. The first time I went to a carnival _____ .

Variation:

You may use the most memorable time instead of the first time.

FANTASY

(Grades 4-12/Ages 9-18)

Objective:

To provide participants a structure for sharing after the getting acquainted has been accomplished

Materials:

☐ Copy of the list of questions (see below) for the leader

Procedure:

This activity is probably best used after the group has established some rapport or met several times. Read each question aloud, allowing two or three students to answer. This will help to maintain participants' interest. Ask the group members the following questions:

If you could be another person, a free spirit, with no responsibilities or duties:

- What would you like to do or be?
- Where would you like to live?
- What hobbies would you like to have?
- What foods would you like to eat?
- What magazines would you like to read?
- What books would you like to read?
- What CDs or tapes would you like to have?
- What kinds of clothes would you like to wear?
- What kind of house would you like to live in?
- What famous people (living or dead) would you like to have as your closest friends?
- Where would you like to travel?
- Who would you like to visit?
- What kind of pet would you like to have?
- How would you like to look?

POSITIVE PARTICIPATION
(Grades 5-12/Ages 10-18)

Objective:

To provide participants an opportunity to get acquainted by sharing only positive activities

Materials:

☐ Instructions (see below) either duplicated for each participant or delivered verbally

Procedure:

Instruct each person to choose a partner whom he/she does not know. Then have them choose a set of partners to make a foursome. If time is short, use only pairs. Explain that each group member has equal time to answer the presented statement. *Note:* The statements may be presented in one session or several sessions. Distribute or read aloud the following positive statements:

PERSONAL ATTRIBUTES

- Two physical qualities I like about myself.
- Two personality qualities I like about myself.
- Two talents or skills I feel good about in myself.

ACTIVITY ACHIEVEMENTS

- My two most satisfying achievements.
- My two most growth-producing relationships.

SITUATIONS

- Two things I "do" which I feel positive about.
- Two people I feel positive about when I'm with them.
- Two places where I feel positive.

SHARE A SITUATION

- A time in your past when you felt you were at your best.

REFOCUS

- Tell your partner one physical feature you like about him/her.
- Tell your partner one personality trait you like about him/her.
- Tell your partner one talent or skill you like about him/her.
- Share with your partner one positive thing that you are feeling towards him/her at the present time.

SCAVENGER HUNT

(Grades 6-12/Ages 11-18)

Objective:

To assist the group members in getting acquainted

Materials:

☐ Copy of *Scavenger Hunt* (see below) and a pencil for each participant

Procedure:

Distribute a copy of the *Scavenger Hunt* and a pencil to each student. Tell the students to find a group member to fit each description and write the person's name on the line after the category.

SCAVENGER HUNT

LOOK FOR A PERSON:

1. Whose first name starts with the same letter as yours? _____
2. Who enjoys watching baseball on TV? _____
3. Who has never been outside the United States? _____
4. Who was born outside the United States? _____
5. Whose hair color is the same as yours? _____
6. Who is taller than you? _____
7. Who speaks more than one language? _____
8. Whose birthday month is the same as yours? _____
9. Who has a dog? _____
10. Who has the same hobby as you do? _____
11. Who does not have a middle name? _____
12. Who has the same number of siblings as you? _____
13. Whose favorite color is purple? _____
14. Whose father or mother is a teacher? _____
15. Who likes to water ski? _____
16. Who was born in this state? _____
17. Who wears the same size shoe as you? _____
18. Who has the same favorite TV show as you? _____
19. Who was born in the same state as you? _____
20. Who plays a musical instrument? _____

GET-ACQUAINTED BINGO

(Grades 6-12/Ages 11-18)

Objective:

To structure a way for participants to get better acquainted and to promote assertive behavior

Materials:

☐ Copy of *Get-Acquainted Bingo* (page 53) and a pencil for each participant

Procedure:

Distribute a copy of *Get-Acquainted Bingo* and a pencil to each student. (If you prefer to make your own bingo sheet, you may substitute more localized activities or places.) Set a limited time (about 10 minutes) for the students to go around the room, find a person who fits the clue, and have him/her sign the sheet. One person may sign one block per card—no repetitions are allowed.

When a row on the sheet has been completed either vertically, horizontally, or diagonally, the owner should yell, "BINGO." A small prize or privilege may be appropriate for this occasion. If time permits, you may continue until someone has completed the entire sheet which will require special recognition or a special prize.

GET-ACQUAINTED BINGO

IS NEW TO THE GROUP	LIVED NEAR THE BEACH	LIKES TO READ	WAS BORN OUTSIDE THE U.S.A.	CAN ICE SKATE
FAVORITE COLOR IS BLUE	LIKES TO COOK	HAS A LARGE FAMILY (5 OR MORE)	PLAYS A MUSICAL INSTRUMENT	IS LEFT-HANDED
GREW UP IN THE COUNTRY	LIKES ROCK AND ROLL	YOUR OWN NAME	CAN HOP ON ONE FOOT	CAN TAP DANCE
HAS A NEW OUTFIT	HAS A DOG	WAS BORN WITHIN 10 DAYS OF CHRISTMAS	LIVED IN A LARGE CITY	FAVORITE FOOD IS PIZZA
IS AN ARTIST	GOES TO MOVIES ONCE A WEEK	HAS A BROTHER	LIKES CLASSICAL MUSIC	WAS BORN IN THE SUMMER

TOILET PAPER

(Grades 7-Adult/Ages 12 and up)

Objective:

To structure a method of participants getting to know each other better

Materials:

☐ Roll of toilet paper

Procedure:

Instruct each member of the group to pull off a section of toilet paper the size they normally use. (Not knowing the purpose of the paper, participants will pull off a variety of sizes which will make the activity more interesting.) Then ask the participants to tell a fact about their life for each square of toilet paper they are holding.

When each member of the group has shared his/her list of facts, process the activity by asking for things they found in common. Offer an opportunity for members to ask questions of each other about something they heard, allowing the person being questioned the option of answering or not answering personal questions.

Alternatives:

By changing the directions, this activity can also be used for friendship, anger-management, character-education, or study-skills lessons. Participants may name friendship qualities, anger-management techniques, character traits they possess, or study-skills techniques.

TOOLS
FOR

ENCOURAGING
FEELINGS
COMMUNICATION

MY WORD
(Grades 1-8/Ages 6-13)

Objective:

To increase the vocabulary of the students with positive words and relate the words to a positive feeling experience during the day

Materials:

☐ Container, basket, or can; slips of paper, marker

Procedure:

Write age-appropriate words (see *Positive Words* below for suggestions) on the slips of paper and put them in a container, basket, or can. Have at least one slip of paper for each student. Some words may be written more than once. Place the container in a convenient place so that it is easily accessible on entry into the room. Have the students quietly draw a word and place it in their desks, pockets, or some place where they can look at it frequently during the day. At the close of the day, have them share ways their word related to the experiences of the day. This sharing can be done with the whole class, in small groups, or in pairs.

POSITIVE WORDS

happy	liking	open
validating	supportive	humorous
joyous	giving	accepting
enthusiastic	communicating	reinforcing
optimistic	contented	stroking
OK	loving	super
listening	trusting	fun
friendly	involved	thrilled
understanding	relaxed	pleasing
fantastic	responsive	authentic
delightful	positive	sincere
exciting	gentle	helping
believing	praising	comfortable
creative	forgiving	encouraging
genuine	kind	great
spontaneous	good	rejoicing
respecting	caring	cheery

FINDING FEELINGS

(Grades K-8/Ages 5-13)

Objective:

To assist group members in identifying a variety of feelings by looking at outward expressions

Materials:

☐ Magazines, gluestick, scissors, a sheet of construction paper, and a pencil (optional) for each participant

Procedure:

In order to encourage participants' sensitivity in recognizing feelings, instruct them to find pictures in magazines which express feelings. Distribute magazines, scissors, a gluestick, construction paper, and a pencil (if appropriate for the age of the group members) to each participant. Instruct them to cut out feeling pictures and glue the pictures on a sheet of construction paper. Then have the participants identify each feeling by writing the feeling words below the pictures on the paper or discussing the meaning of the pictures in small groups. Encourage them to discuss when each feeling is appropriate. For example: When my dog died, I felt sad. Help them separate feelings from behavior and understand the use of appropriate behavior to accompany the feeling.

FEELING STORIES

(Grades 3-12/Ages 8-18)

Objective:

To increase participants' understanding of feelings and the reaction patterns to events which provoke different feelings

Materials:

☐ Several copies of *Feelings Heard in the Story* (see below), a pencil, and paper for each participant

Procedure:

Distribute a piece of paper and a pencil to each participant. Instruct the participants to write a list of events which cause them to experience different feelings and identify one or two feelings for each event listed. Next they should look at the list of feelings, choose one or two, and write a story about the event which provoked that feeling. The story should include: the event, the feelings, and some description about how the feelings relate to the event.

When the stories are complete, distribute a copy of *Feelings Heard in the Story* to each participant. Have them move into small groups for sharing or read the stories in front of the whole group on a voluntary basis. Tell the participants to listen to the story being read and identify the author and the feelings heard in the story on the *Feelings Heard in the Story* sheet. Then have them give the sheets to the author for confirmation of the feelings heard. *Note:* If this activity is being presented in a classroom, decide on the number of sheets to be filled out for each student and assign that number of students to complete the task. **Warning!** Group members should share feelings only on a voluntary basis. Never force anyone to participate in a feeling-related experience.

FEELINGS HEARD IN THE STORY

Author _____

Feelings Heard in the Story

_____   _____

_____   _____

_____   _____

_____   _____

Name _____

MASKS OF FEELINGS

(Grades 3-8/Ages 8-13)

Objective:

To help participants identify feelings and discuss the ways used to mask feelings so that other people will not detect them

Materials:

- ☐ Basket or box
- ☐ Flat stick such as a popsicle stick, scissors, heavy paper, markers, and gluestick for each participant

Procedure:

Distribute a flat stick, scissors, heavy paper, markers, and gluestick to each participant. Tell them to make masks out of heavy paper illustrating facial expressions showing specific feelings. When the participants have finished drawing, instruct them to cut out their masks and glue them to the flat stick. Place the masks in the basket/box. Have each person draw one mask from the basket/box, identify the feeling represented on the mask, and describe a time when he/she had that feeling.

Variations:

Have the participants write a story about the feeling shown on the mask. This can be easily incorporated into a writing session. The exercise can be repeated again by drawing a different mask each day and writing about the feeling, resulting in a notebook of feeling stories. *Note:* Students can use the notebook of feelings for the class library by including each person's stories.

Participants may also talk about times when their expression did not match their internal feelings; such as when they are very sad inside, or when they laugh too much to cover up their anger. Have them discuss covering feelings by not expressing them.

FEELING CARDS

(Grades 2-8/Ages 7-13)

Objective:

To help participants identify feelings and how they relate to events

Materials:

☐ 3" x 5" cards

Procedure:

Write a feeling word or draw a picture depicting a feeling on half of the 3" x 5" cards. Write or draw illustrations of events on the remaining cards. Make a pile of feelings cards and a pile of events cards. Select a participant to draw one card from the feeling stack and one card from the event stack. If the person can explain how the event would produce the feeling, a match is made and he/she keeps the cards. If a match is not made, the cards are returned to the bottom of their respective piles. Select another participant, and repeat the procedure until the allotted time has elapsed.

Suggested words and events are:

FEELINGS	EVENTS
Sad	Friends hurt in an automobile accident
Elated	Passed an important test
Disappointed	Not selected for the basketball team
Disgusted	Dropped notebook in hall, papers spilled
Excited	Planning a trip to Disneyworld
Afraid	Asked to make a speech in the school play
Pressured	Too much homework
Thoughtful	Brought some flowers to my teacher
Rebellious	Tired of being told what to do
Cooperative	Working with the team to win the tournament
Critical	Nobody ever seems to get anything right
Accepting	New student seems to fit in well
Embarrassed	Teachers called on me and I didn't know the answer.
Cherished	Grandmother called for Valentine's Day
Missed	The class welcomed me back after an illness
Appreciated	Parents liked it when I cleaned up my room
Ashamed	Forgot to do my homework
Surprised	Made better grade on the paper than I expected

Add as many *Feelings/Events* as you like. More mature group members will enjoy making the card game themselves.

IMAGINARY BOX

(Grades 3-Adult/Ages 8 and up)

Objective:

To help participants throw away negatives, obstacles, or conflicts in order to promote positive thinking

Materials:

None.

Procedure:

This exercise can be used as a successful starter before brainstorming in problem solving. It can also be used in groups as an ice breaker.

Have the group participants seated with their feet flat on the floor. Ask them to imagine that there is a sizable cardboard box placed on their laps. Next say:

> "With your eyes closed feel the box up and down the sides to see how big it is. Open the box with your hands. Pull back the flaps and keep the box open. Now reach up to your head and pull out all the negative 'stuff' you have stored there—all the road blocks—the 'why it can't be done.' Keep pulling these things out and stuffing them in the box. If you continue pulling, your box may be nearly full. When you think you are rid of most of this baggage, quickly close the box so that none of it will escape. Fold the box tops down and overlap them so that they will stay in place. Set this box down on the floor near your chair. Now we can proceed with the tasks we want to work on today."

Some discussion may be initiated if this is the only activity performed by the group. Begin with such questions as:

> "What did you put in your box which you think would interfere significantly with what we do today?"

Be sure everyone feels free to choose to participate. Discussion is not recommended to introduce a definite problem since negatives can be a distraction from getting into the real issue.

MAINTAINING MY PACKAGE

(Grades 4-Adult/Ages 9 and up)

Objective:

To help participants in maintaining their self-esteem by describing it as their "package"

Materials:

- ☐ Box wrapped as a package
- ☐ Picture of a package (see sample below) on 11 x 8½ paper and a pencil for each participant

Procedure:

Show the wrapped box to the participants. Ask them to guess what is inside the box. After several guesses, explain that there is no way to tell what is inside the box without opening it and seeing what is inside. Continue the discussion by telling the participants that the are like the package—they have many feelings and thoughts inside them that are unknown unless they open up their "package." Distribute the picture of a package and a pencil to each participant. Then have them write the following on the package:

- A. Places where you feel that you belong.
- B. People who love you unconditionally.
- C. Things that you can do that make you feel competent.
- D. Ways you know to make friends.
- E. Ways you have learned to "go with the flow." (Be flexible.)
- F. Ways you have learned to "hang in." (Stick with the task.)
- G. Ways you value your "inner wisdom."
- H. Ways you forgive yourself when you make a mistake.

Have the group members share their answers. This may take several sessions. At the end of the group, have the participants make a phrase which enhances self-esteem and repeat it together. Example: I am a valuable and worthwhile person. Continue the discussion by having the participants share what it takes to crumple their package.

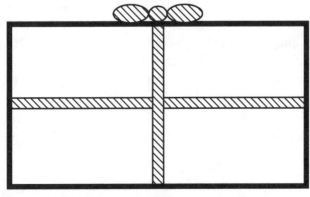

LEARNING TO LISTEN

(Grades 4-12/Ages 9-18)

Objective:

To teach the participant some basic listening skills that will enhance relationships in a group and be of use later in life

Materials:

☐ Copy of *Reflecting Feelings* (page 65) and a pencil for each participant

Procedure:

Discuss the importance of learning to listen by reviewing the following:

1. "How do you know when someone is listening?"

   • They look at you.
   • They nod.
   • They lean forward.
   • Their faces show some response.
   • They may say something in response.

2. "What do they say that makes you know that they heard you?"

   • They may repeat what you said.
   • Their remarks are related to what you said.
   • They get the facts accurately.
   • They seem to understand how you feel.

Next, tell the participants they are going to practice a way of listening which will help them to better understand the person who is talking. Then say:

> "When someone seems to understand how you feel, he/she may say so by trying to interpret the feeling you seem to be expressing. You can do this by starting your sentence with "You feel_____," or some variation of that statement. For example: "I'm not sure I want to go to the fifth grade." The response might be, "You feel uncertain because you are not sure you will be happy there." When you, as a listener, reflect a feeling back to the speaker it indicates that you really heard him/her.

Distribute a copy of *Reflecting Feelings* and a pencil to each participant. Instruct them to complete the activity sheet and, when finished, be prepared to share their answers with the group.

REFLECTING FEELINGS

1. **I just don't like Mary. I am going to tell the teacher how she is acting.**
   You feel _____
   because _____

2. **I hope that Sam doesn't sit by me on the bus. He is so obnoxious.**
   You feel _____
   because _____

3. **My brother is so bad in school. He just bothers everyone all the time.**
   You feel _____
   because _____

4. **My teacher gives impossible homework assignments.**
   You feel _____
   because _____

5. **Bob cuts up in our group so much that I wish he would quit.**
   You feel _____
   because _____

6. **Sometimes I wish that my sister would get lost somewhere.**
   You feel _____
   because _____

7. **This work is so hard. I don't think I will ever get finished.**
   You feel _____
   because _____

8. **That is the worst class. I wish I didn't have to go.**
   You feel _____
   because _____

9. **This old shirt is so ugly. I think I'll throw it away.**
   You feel _____
   because _____

Apply these skills of listening in your everyday life.

ONE WORD COMMUNICATION

(Grades 4-Adult/Ages 9 and up)

Objective:

To help members of the group learn to express themselves directly and distinctly with clarity of feeling

Materials:

☐ Copy of *One Word Communication* (See below) and a pencil for each participant

Procedure:

Distribute a copy of *One Word Communication* and a pencil to each participant. Have the group members divide into pairs. Instruct the pairs to go to a quiet place and designate which person will go first. The person going first should read the first statement on the list. The other person should state a one-word feeling which the first person records on his/her paper. When the first list is completed, the procedure is repeated with the participants changing roles. The activity continues until the second list is complete. The lists are then given to the person whose answers are on the paper. Then have the participants discuss the experience and their related feelings.

ONE WORD COMMUNICATION

The current situation _____

Their friends _____

The other person _____

Their achievements _____

The way they feel _____

Their appearance _____

Their personal history _____

Their name _____

Their address _____

Their family _____

Their skills _____

Their intelligence _____

Their faith _____

Their attitude _____

Their values _____

Their country _____

Their patriotism _____

Their sense of justice _____

Their sense of maturity _____

Their sense of humor _____

SIGNIFICANT STROKES

(Grades 4-Adult/Ages 9 and up)

Objective:

To help participants identify persons from whom they get significant positive reinforcement and identify what it is that they need from those persons

Materials:

☐ Copy of *Significant Strokes* (see below) and a pencil for each participant

Procedure:

Distribute a copy of *Significant Strokes* and a pencil to each participant. Tell the participants to name the person who delivers the most strokes (reinforcements) to them. This can be generalized in terms such as: my boss, my teacher, my parents, my principal, my husband, etc.

Have the participants identify the kinds of strokes received, either verbal or non-verbal, and describe the responses which they give to positive strokes. Then ask them to describe the kinds of strokes they return to a person and the response which they receive. Conclude the activity by asking for a show of hands from those participants who believe it is easier to respond with a positive stroke if positive strokes have been received.

SIGNIFICANT STROKES

Name _____

Person who gives me positive strokes _____

Kinds of strokes received _____

_____

_____

Responses I give to these strokes _____

_____

_____

Strokes I give to this person _____

_____

_____

Responses this person gives me _____

_____

_____

ALL ABOUT ME

(Grades 2-5/Ages 7-10)

Objective:

To teach participants to use descriptive language in verbalization, to share with others and to listen carefully to others (This exercise will also be helpful in building team spirit and understanding.)

Materials:

☐ Paper and a pencil or crayons for each participant

Procedure:

Distribute a piece of paper and a pencil or crayons to each participant. Instruct them divide the paper into quarters and, in each square, write or draw one of the following:

ALL ABOUT THE WAY I LOOK	ALL ABOUT THE PLACE I LIVE
ALL ABOUT THE PEOPLE WHO LIVE AT MY HOUSE	ALL ABOUT MY FAVORITE THING TO DO

Explain that this activity will be a way for them to learn about themselves and others in the group. Instruct the participants to draw or write about each topic in the designated square. When everyone has finished drawing, ask the participants to talk about what they have written or drawn in the squares. Instruct the other group members to listen very carefully so that when the speaker is finished, the listeners can tell you what they heard.

As each person finishes telling about his/her sheet, ask for immediate feedback from the group. Then have the speaker verify the accuracy of the listeners.

MY MOST EXCITING ADVENTURE

(Grades K-Adult/Ages 5 and up)

Objective:

To increase participants' awareness of feelings and to learn to share the good experiences of others

Materials:

☐ Container (box or basket)
☐ Slip of paper and a pencil for each participant

Procedure:

Distribute a slip of paper and a pencil to each participant. Have each participant write his/her name on the slip of paper, fold it, and place the paper in the container. Tell the participants that they are going to talk about exciting things which they have experienced or done. These are things that make them feel good. Begin modeling by telling them an exciting thing that you, as the leader, have experienced.

Then draw a name out of the container to decide who will be next. As each participant completes his/her own story, draw the name of the next storyteller. Remind the participants that they may say "I pass" if they prefer not to participate.

If you have a large group or a whole classroom, you may the divide the participants into pairs to experience the sharing. When everyone has finished sharing, ask the participants to identify the feelings they experienced while telling their stories.

MY SUCCESS RECORD

(Grades 1-8/Ages 6-13)

Objective:

To help participants become aware of successes in order to increase their own opportunity for success and raise their self-esteem

Materials:

☐ Copy of *My Success Record* (see below) and a pencil for each participant

Procedure:

Explain to the participants that it is important that they become aware of their successes. Distribute a copy of *My Success Record* and a pencil to each participant. Tell the participants to record the acts they perform that they feel are successful during the day. Set a time for them to come back and report in. For younger children the time should be short—maybe a half day or at most a whole day. Later this can be extended to a week. Send the records home at the end of the week with positive comments. Be sure the participants do not set goals for success that are so high they are unreachable, causing them to become discouraged. Remember: Short steps of progress will encourage and motivate.

MY SUCCESS RECORD

DATE	MY SUCCESSES
Monday	
Tuesday	
Wednesday	
Thursday	
Friday	
Saturday	
Sunday	

MY SUCCESS CHART

(Grades 3-12/Ages 8-18)

Objective:

To teach participants to identify their successes and to increase their ability in self- reinforcement

Materials:

☐ Copy of *My Success Chart* (see below) and a pencil for each participant

Procedure:

Ask the participants to define *success*. If necessary, look the word up in a dictionary. Distribute a copy of *My Success Chart* and a pencil to each participant. Explain the chart and instruct them to complete it.

When the charts have been completed, have each person share his/her success story. If time is limited, have them choose only one of their successes in order to give each person time to share their *dream success*. Conclude the activity by letting the group brainstorm about ways they can influence their dreams to come true.

MY SUCCESS CHART

	WHERE (Identify location)	WHAT (Describe the event)	WHY (Why it was a success?)
Home			
School			
Sports			
Other			
My Dream Success			

SWEET TO MY EAR

(Grades 4-12/Ages 9-18)

Objective:

To assist participants in identifying positive words which they like to hear and to encourage the use of those words when commanding others

Materials:

- ☐ Bulletin board and pins (optional)
- ☐ 8 slips of paper, colored construction paper, a gluestick, and a pencil for each participant

Procedure:

Distribute eight slips of paper, colored construction paper, a gluestick, and a pencil to each participant. Instruct the participants to write one adjective which describes them on each slip of paper. Examples of adjectives:

- Handsome or Ugly
- Funny or Dull
- Intelligent or Stupid
- Kind or Unthoughtful

When the participants have finished writing, ask them to arrange the words in order of their pleasure in hearing the words as commendations. The most desirable word is at the top. Ask them to lay aside any words which they would like to change about themselves.

Have the participants form pairs and read the words to each other with whatever comments they would like to make. Examples of comments:

- I think I am dependable because I always turn my homework in on time.
- I think I am irresponsible because I always forget to do my chores at home.

Tell the participants to write their names on the construction paper and glue the positive words on the paper. If you choose to, post the papers on a bulletin board to remind the group members that these are commendations which they like to hear.

Ask the participants to discuss ways they can use these words to commend others. For example:

- I like the way you dress—your clothes always look so nice.
- You are so smart—you always seem to understand the lessons.

If there are words they don't like, ask them to devise ways to change their behavior which would eliminate those words from their vocabulary. For example:

- I would like to be more careful about getting my homework in.
- I want to remember my chores at home.

MIRROR, MIRROR ON THE WALL

(Grades 3-8/Ages 8-13)

Objective:

To help participants in self-discovery reinforced by positive feedback

Materials:

- ☐ Full length mirror, flipchart and marker or chalkboard and chalk
- ☐ 2 pieces of art paper, crayons or markers, and a pencil for each participant

Procedure:

Distribute two pieces of art paper, crayons or markers, and a pencil to each participant. Instruct each person to draw a picture of him/herself. While they are drawing, write the following questions on the flipchart or chalkboard:

- • In what ways are we alike?
- • In what ways are we different?
- • What things do we see that we like about ourselves?
- • What do we know about each other that the mirror does not show?

After the drawings are completed, tell the group members choose partners. Have the partners stand together in front of the mirror, tell what they see, and answer the questions on the flipchart/chalkboard.

Next, instruct the partners to draw pictures of each other. While they are drawing, write the following questions on the flipchart/chalkboard:

- • How was the self portrait like the one drawn by your partner?
- • How was it different?
- • What did you learn about your partner by drawing the picture?
- • What have you learned from this activity?

When the participants have finished drawing, have them compare these portraits with the original ones they drew of themselves and answer the questions on the flipchart/chalkboard.

Because there is limited space at the mirror, you may need to assign this activity to one small group at a time.

DESIGN A T-SHIRT

(Grades 4-Adult/Ages 9 and up)

Objective:

To raise awareness of themes that run through the lives of the participants

Materials:

☐ Paper, a pencil, and crayons or markers for each participant

Procedure:

Ask the participants to close their eyes and imagine that they have just gotten a job as a designer of T-shirts. Their first assignment is to design a shirt about themselves. Tell the participants to review their lives and decide what theme would be most descriptive. Distribute paper, a pencil, and crayons or markers to each participant. Have them draw and label the design for their T-shirts. When everyone has finished designing their shirts, have the participants share their designs with the group and explain the reason for their choice.

Variations:

Have the group participants close their eyes and imagine that a Hollywood movie producer wants to make a movie of their lives. Review what has happened from birth until now. What would be the title of the movie?

Have the group participants close their eyes and imagine that a famous author of biographies wants to write the story of their lives. Think over the years which they have lived already. What would be the title of the book?

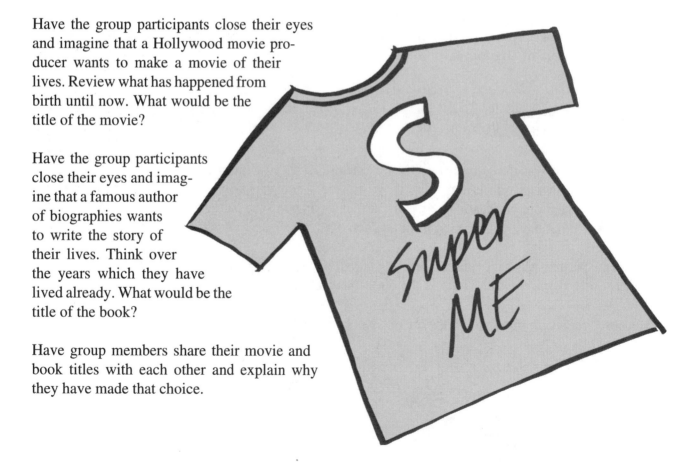

Have group members share their movie and book titles with each other and explain why they have made that choice.

I BETCHA DIDN'T KNOW

(Grades 3-Adult/Ages 8 and up)

Objective:

To help participants get acquainted and encourage communication (This exercise can provide some humor as well as information about each participant.)

Materials:

None.

Procedure:

Have the participants sit in a circle. Tell the group members to think of something about themselves which most people don't know, a kind of surprise. Have the leader begin by sharing something about him/herself as a model. For example:

- I betcha didn't know that I used to be a painter and that I have done many paintings.
- I betcha didn't know that I have a big sister who is a teacher.
- I betcha didn't know that I used to live in Alaska.
- I betcha didn't know that I like to write poems.
- I betcha didn't know that my dad is an oceanographer.

Let each participant take a turn as he/she thinks of something to say. Tell them to start each revelation with "I betcha didn't know_____." Give the participants time to respond to each other.

When everyone has had a turn, process what has been learned. Discuss whether or not that knowledge makes any difference in their relationships to the members of the group.

SECRET ENCOURAGEMENT
(Grades 4-Adult/Ages 9 and up)

Objective:

To teach group members to give positive reinforcement and to learn to be gracious receivers of compliments

Materials:

☐ Large card or 8" x 10" piece of paper, pins, and crayons or pencils for each participant

Procedure:

After the group has had some time to get acquainted, perhaps several sessions, give each group member a piece of paper to pin on the back of another member. When everyone has a paper on his/her back, ask the participants to circulate and write one thing they like about that person on each paper. This may take 5-15 minutes, depending on the size of the group. When everyone has written on each person's paper, stop the group, and let the participants unpin the papers. Give the owners time to read the papers silently. Ask for any expression of feelings.

Give the participants a chance to read their papers aloud to the group. Then discuss the difference in being a giver and a receiver of compliments. Ask which was harder, writing on the paper or reading one's own paper aloud. Discuss the possible responses a person can give when receiving compliments.

CARD FILE

(Grades 4-12/Ages 9-18)

Objective:

To increase participants' self awareness and encourage communication in the group

Materials:

☐ Six 7" x 9" cards and a pencil or crayons for each participant

Procedure:

Distribute six cards and a pencil or crayons to each participant. On each card, ask them to draw one of the following:

1. Two things you do well.

2. A favorite place you like to be.

3. Your greatest achievement.

4. Your favorite dream of the future.

5. Two people who are most important to you.

6. Three words you would like to have said about you.

When the participants have finished drawing, ask them to show their cards and explain any unclear statements. Discuss the similarities and differences between the participants' responses. Encourage the group members to file their cards and add to them as they make new discoveries about themselves.

Alternative:

Have the participants draw on one card at each session and make a file of them for the end of the series of meetings. This activity can serve as an icebreaker or as closure for a long series of group meetings.

BIRTHDAY CANDLES

(Grades 4-8/Ages 9-13)

Objective:

To enhance participants' communication and encourage verbalization

Materials:

☐ Picture of a birthday cake with candles or a real birthday cake with candles may be used then served as a refreshment at the end of the group, flipchart and marker or chalkboard and chalk

Procedure:

Show the group members the birthday cake with candles. Ask them to think of one wish they would make if they were blowing out their birthday candles. (If you are using a real cake, you may allow each person to pull and blow out one candle after his/her turn.) Then ask each group member to share his/her wish and complete the following statements:

- My wish about home is …

- My wish about school is …

- My wish about me is …

After everyone has had a turn, discuss the participants' wishes, their similarities and differences. On the flipchart/chalkboard, make a list of the wishes that are possible and those that seem unrealistic. Of the possible ones, suggest some ways in which the person who made the wish can begin making it come true.

SPOTLIGHTING

(Grades 4-Adult/Ages 9 and up)

Objective:

To teach participants to give and receive positive statements

Materials:

☐ 3" x 5" card and a pencil for each participant

Procedure:

Ask the group members to sit in a circle. Distribute a 3" x 5" card and a pencil to each participant. Instruct each participant to write at the top of the card his/her name and one positive adjective to describe him/herself. For example:

Ann Parker   Industrious   Creative   ....

Tom Harmon   Intelligent   Polite   ....

Then have each participant pass his/her card to the person on his/her right, who then writes one positive adjective about the person whose name is on the card. Continue the procedure passing the card all the way around the circle until it comes back to the owner. At that point, the card should contain an adjective from each member of the group.

Beginning with one person, have that person tell what adjective he/she used to describe him/herself and why. Then pass the card around the group, giving each person time to tell what adjective he/she put on the card and why. Ask each person to speak directly to the person being "spotlighted" using his/her name. For example:

- "Ann, you are industrious because you work hard and try to do a good job."
- "Ann, I said that you are creative because you do all those jobs with a special flare."
- "Tom, you are intelligent because you seem to understand both math and science."
- "Tom, I think you are polite because you are very nice to everybody."

Continue this procedure until each person's card has been passed around the group. Try to encourage people to give adjectives that relate to personality traits rather than looks. This exercise is intended to be used with a group who is well acquainted. It makes an effective closing as the group comes to an end.

I AM

(Grades 6-Adult/Ages 11 and up)

Objective:

To increase participants' self-awareness and encourage communication

Materials:

☐ Copy of *I Am* (page 83) and a pencil for each participant

Procedure:

Discuss the importance of knowing oneself and learning to communicate that self to others in an acceptable manner. Distribute a copy of *I Am* and a pencil to each participant. Explain the concept of using the continuum with the extreme left being a definite "not at all" and the extreme right being a definite "very much." Then instruct the participants to make a check mark on the continuum line indicating their rating of themselves. If necessary, explain any unclear words to insure that everyone has the same concept of the word meaning.

Conclude the activity by having the participants share any pertinent information or conclusions about their completed activity sheets.

This exercise can also be turned into a follow-up entitled *I Would Like To Be*. Have the participants use the same continuum and mark it with a different symbol or colored pencils to indicate how they would like to be. Follow up with a discussion of ways they can make changes in themselves and the things they may need to accept as unchangeable. For example:

I WOULD LIKE TO BE

	NOT AT ALL	VERY MUCH
Athletic	|---|---|✖|---|---|---|---|---|---|
Attractive	|---|---|---|---|✖|---|---|---|---|
Passive	|---|---|---|---|---|---|---|✖|---|
Confident	|---|---|---|✖|---|---|---|---|---|

I AM

NOT AT ALL   VERY MUCH

Athletic	|---|---|---|---|---|---|---|---|---|
Attractive	|---|---|---|---|---|---|---|---|---|
Passive (indifferent)	|---|---|---|---|---|---|---|---|---|
Confident	|---|---|---|---|---|---|---|---|---|
Dependable	|---|---|---|---|---|---|---|---|---|
Agile	|---|---|---|---|---|---|---|---|---|
Open	|---|---|---|---|---|---|---|---|---|
Goal-directed	|---|---|---|---|---|---|---|---|---|
Aimless	|---|---|---|---|---|---|---|---|---|
Sociable	|---|---|---|---|---|---|---|---|---|
A Leader	|---|---|---|---|---|---|---|---|---|
Happy	|---|---|---|---|---|---|---|---|---|
Hostile	|---|---|---|---|---|---|---|---|---|
Helpful	|---|---|---|---|---|---|---|---|---|
Honest	|---|---|---|---|---|---|---|---|---|
Independent	|---|---|---|---|---|---|---|---|---|
Hypocritical	|---|---|---|---|---|---|---|---|---|
Secure	|---|---|---|---|---|---|---|---|---|
Popular	|---|---|---|---|---|---|---|---|---|
Sad	|---|---|---|---|---|---|---|---|---|
Scatterbrained	|---|---|---|---|---|---|---|---|---|
Sensible	|---|---|---|---|---|---|---|---|---|
Shy	|---|---|---|---|---|---|---|---|---|
Sensitive	|---|---|---|---|---|---|---|---|---|
Sincere	|---|---|---|---|---|---|---|---|---|
Coordinated	|---|---|---|---|---|---|---|---|---|
Responsible	|---|---|---|---|---|---|---|---|---|
Motivated	|---|---|---|---|---|---|---|---|---|
Lazy	|---|---|---|---|---|---|---|---|---|

MY WELL

(Grades 2-5/Ages 7-10)

Objective:

To assist the participants in self reinforcement by increasing awareness of the learning skills

Materials:

- ☐ Slips of paper
- ☐ Aluminum can, construction paper, markers, and a gluestick for each participant

Procedure:

Distribute an aluminum can, construction paper, markers, and a gluestick to each participant. Instruct them to decorate the can and label it "My Well." Show the participants the slips of paper and tell them as they learn new skills they should write the skill on the paper and place it in the can. On Friday or at a regularly appointed time, have them pour out the pieces of paper and review the kinds of skills they have learned. (**Caution:** Regularly emphasize to the participants that what is important is not how many skills they learn, but learning more each week. If this is not emphasized, the classmates may become too competitive and the activity becomes self-defeating.

TOOLS
FOR

FINDING
SOLUTIONS

BRAINSTORMING

(Grades 4-Adult/Ages 9 and up)

Objective:

To encourage respect for creative abilities in problem solving

Materials:

☐ Large flipchart and marker or chalkboard and chalk

Procedure:

Choose a specific task which has interest for most of the group. Introduce brainstorming by pointing out that you are looking for ideas to solve a particular issue. For example:

- Working out playground rules
- Working out classroom discussion procedures
- Determining ways to provide some free time for the faculty at lunch
- Deciding about the spring picnic
- Determining the procedure for morning check-in
- Deciding a method for clean-up in the afternoon

Explain to the participants that the basic rule is to generate as many ideas as possible in a short period, without evaluation or discussion. All ideas are included even though they may seem illogical or ridiculous. After the list is complete, each idea will be evaluated.

As the ideas are contributed, write them on the chalkboard/flipchart. Use approximately five minutes for the brainstorming. Number the items to see how many possible solutions are given. Then ask:

"Did everyone have a chance to contribute an idea?"
"Did you avoid criticizing or evaluating contributions?"

Then go back and cross off all the impossible ideas. Discuss the possibilities and consequences of the remaining ideas, reducing the list to two or three realistic possible solutions. Decide on a first choice. Keep the second and third choices to use in the event the first choice does not succeed. Select a planning committee to begin the implementation of the ideas.

This activity can be used frequently and very helpfully to enrich decisions and teach respect, and works well in small or large groups.

GOAL SETTING

(Grades 4-12/Ages 9-18)

Objective:

To encourage goal setting as a way of accomplishing a task

Materials:

☐ Copy of *Goal Sheet* (page 89) and a pencil for each participant

Procedure:

Discuss the meaning and importance of goal-setting by asking the participants the following questions:

- What is a goal? (A limit, boundary, set place or direction, point of success)

- Why is it important to set goals? (To direct our energies, motivate achievement, determine values, provide direction, have something to work for, stay on track, determine what is really important)

- What are some obstacles that get in the way of achieving our goals? (Bad habits, misperceptions, fears, assumptions, impatience, resistance to change)

- What is the criteria for a good goal? (It is conceivable—can be put into words, it is possible, controllable—includes others with permission, measurable—able to know when it was (wasn't) accomplished, definite—no "either-or"

Distribute a copy of the *Goal Sheet* and a pencil to each person and instruct them to complete it. Then have the participants discuss their goals with the group. Set a definite time for a report-in on goal achievement. This review should include progress on the goal and resetting goals which were not accomplished. If it is necessary to reset a goal, review the criteria for a good goal, and be sure any new goal meets those criteria.

GOAL SHEET

My Goal for:

Today/Tomorrow _____

Next week/Next month _____

Next year _____

Five/Ten years _____

✳ REMEMBER ✳

Goals must be
REALISTIC—— MANAGEABLE——FLEXIBLE
Goals must be
OBSERVABLE AND MEASURABLE

Write your most important immediate goal _____

_____

Write several ways you can reach your goal _____

_____

_____

Select your most reasonable choice _____

_____

Plan how you can put your goal in operation _____

_____

_____

Explain how will you know when your goal is achieved _____

_____

Who can you count on for help/support _____

_____

LISTENING VOCABULARY

(Grades 2-12/Ages 7-18)

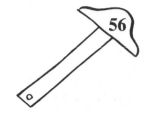

Objective:

To increase the feeling vocabulary of participants and to facilitate identifying and expressing feelings

Materials:

☐ List of feeling words (see below); bulletin board, poster, or flipchart; marker; small pieces of paper or cards (optional); container (optional)

Procedure:

Write a list of feeling words on a bulletin board, poster, or flipchart. When an occasion arises, refer to the list, asking the person to identify his/her feeling by selecting a word from the list. The words can also be placed on small pieces of paper or cards to be drawn out of a container by the participants and used in sentences. With frequent use, the participants will become more comfortable and understand their feelings.

MILD FEELINGS	MODERATE FEELINGS	INTENSE FEELINGS
UPSET	MAD	RAGE
FED UP	INFURIATED	IRATE
DOWN	SORROWFUL	DEJECTED
CONCERNED	GLOOMY	DEPRESSED
SCARED	AFRAID	TERRIFIED
ON EDGE	HORRIFIED	ANXIOUS
TROUBLED	WORRIED	DISORIENTED
PUZZLED	APPREHENSIVE	OUT OF CONTROL
EDGY	UNSURE	DISGUSTED
IMPATIENT	BEWILDERED	GUILTY
DISTRUSTFUL	NERVOUS	JEALOUS
SORRY	UPTIGHT	ELATED
DISTURBED	FRUSTRATED	IDOLIZED
HESITANT	REGRETFUL	LOVED
RELUCTANT	ASHAMED	DEDICATED
GOOD	SKEPTICAL	INVIGORATED
CHEERFUL	TURNED OFF	BRAVE
INFATUATED	HAPPY	
WARM	THRILLED	
OK	AFFECTIONATE	
CONFIDENT	CAPABLE	
SAFE	SECURE	
ENERGETIC	ENLIVENED	
PERCEPTIVE	UNDERSTANDING	
CONTENTED	PEACEFUL	

DECISION MAKING

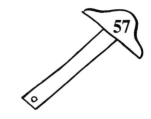

(Grades 4-12/Ages 9-18)

Objective:

To raise participants' awareness of decision making as a part of life

Materials:

☐ Paper and a pencil for each participant

Procedure:

Distribute paper and a pencil to each participant. Ask them to write down at least a dozen decisions which they made yesterday. Remind them of simple decisions such as:

- What to wear
- What to eat for breakfast
- To brush teeth
- What time to leave
- To take books home
- To hand in homework
- To speak to a new participant
- To take a new course next quarter
- To decide where to go to college
- To take a friend to the dance

After the participants have completed their list, ask them to:

- Count and record the number of decisions they made in a day.
- Put a ✔ by the five most important decisions made during the day.
- Put an ✗ by the decisions which affected others.
- Put a ☆ by the decisions which are long lasting in effect.
- Put an ➜ by the decisions which are immediate.
- Put a ❤ by the decisions which will need patience to develop.

Give the participants time to compare their decisions with other members of the group. Close the session by asking:

"What is the most difficult part of making decisions?"

Lead the group members to an answer that relates to taking responsibility and emphasize the number of decisions that they are responsible for making every day. This activity will be enhanced by using Tool 58 as a follow up.

SIX STEPS TO PROBLEM SOLVING

(Grades 5-Adult/Ages 10 and up)

Objective:

To teach participants a structured process for solving problems

Materials:

☐ Copy of *Problem-Solving Model* (page 93) for each participant

Procedure:

Distribute a copy of the *Problem-Solving Model* to each participant and review the information together. Then say:

"Can we agree that all of us have problems, issues, and difficulties to work out all the time and that some of these issues are more important than others? If we learn to work out minor issues, we are more prepared to work out the really big ones when they come along. Let's take a few minutes to look at some possibilities of problems which might affect our entire school" (organization, department, church or group setting in which you are working).

Examples:

- Free lunch time for teachers in an elementary school
- Responsibility for the teacher's lounge
- Assignments for extra duties

- The use of playground equipment by older children
- The disruptions in lunch lines
- Behavior on the school bus

- Break time for employees
- Assignments of desirable vs. undesirable tasks
- Communication concerning company policy

Continue by having the group focus on a group problem or a hypothetical problem which they can process using the *Problem-Solving Model*. If time permits, have each group member take an individual issue and process it through the model. Discuss with the group the importance of having a structured method of problem solving.

PROBLEM-SOLVING MODEL

1. **Admit** you have a **problem**, **conflict**, or **difficultly** in making a decision or planning on a course of action.

2. **Define** your **problem**. (Narrow down the problem area and label it.)

3. **Consider** all your **alternatives** or **choices**. Each one should be weighed against your personal value system as a process of elimination takes place. Choices can be grouped broadly under the following headings:

   a. Confront

   b. Confront and negotiate

   c. "Grin and bear it"

   d. Escape

   e. No choice (Remember—not choosing is a choice.)

4. **Act** on your **choice** or **decision**. Take a risk! At this point you must **consider** all the possible **consequences** of your decision.

5. Be willing to **take** the **consequences**. This helps us to be responsible for our behavior and learn better ways of solving problems in the future.

6. **Rethink** and **redo**. If solutions to a problem are not achieved, or you did not like the consequences, you can usually go back to steps 3 and 4 again and decide differently next time.

PROBLEM-SOLVING EXERCISE

(Grades 5-12/Ages 10-18)

Objective:

To provide a review of actual experiences where the problem-solving model may be applied

Materials:

☐ Prerequisite: Lesson on *Six Steps To Problem Solving* (page 92)

Procedure:

Problem solving is one of the most important skills that a person will ever learn. And practice in problem solving cannot be over emphasized. After the lesson on problem-solving skills, present the group members with one of the problems listed below or one which has come up in the classroom (job, home, etc.).

Suggested problems:

1. Someone teases you.

2. Your dog ran away.

3. You hurt your leg.

4. You broke a glass jar.

5. Your parents are going out for the evening.

6. Your older brother/sister does not want to watch the same TV program you want to watch.

7. You have no one to play with.

8. You are hungry and your mother is busy.

9. Your friend took your football away from you.

10. You lost your homework.

Have the group members add any other problems which they see as pertinent. You may try using one each day as a practice exercise.

TEAM BUILDING

(Grades 4-Adult/Ages 9 and up)

Objective:

To teach participants to accept and cooperate with the decisions of a group or a group member

To learn to create from another's work

Materials:

☐ Paper and pencils or the makings for any project for each group

Procedure:

Divide the participants into small groups. Have each group select a project. One person is assigned to start the project alone without the assistance of other members. At a specified time, another participant takes up the project and works alone without any explanation from the first person. This continues until each group member has had a chance to work on the project.

This same concept can be used in writing a story. Each participant must add to the story as his/her turn comes.

When the project or story has been completed, have a discussion about the feelings of the whole group and each member of the group.

CONFLICT RESOLUTION

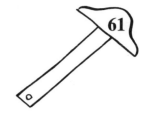

(Grades 5-Adult/Ages 10 and up)

Objective:

To mediate a conflict which may occur between two or more participants or groups

Materials:

☐ Copy of *Conflict Resolution* (page 97)

Procedure:

When a conflict occurs, the following steps can be implemented by a mediator.

1. Have the parties sit opposite each other with the mediator seated nearby. Arrange the seating so that all participants can see each other. The role of the mediator is to arrange the room.

2. Explain the rules. State:

   "You have obviously disagreed about _____*(identify the disagreement).* We have come together to see if we can work this out. I will ask each of you to state your side while the other remains silent. Do not interrupt while someone else is talking. Each person will get a turn. We will begin with sharing what you resent. Let's speak directly using as few words as possible."

3. Begin by calling on the parties one at a time. Listen carefully. Do not allow interruptions from the other party. When the first party has completed his/her statements, turn to the other party for the same response. When they have both finished go on to step 4.

4. Now each of you may ask anything you want of the other person. Have the two parties respond to the requests and tell whether they can honor the request.

5. When some agreement has been reached, ask each party to share something positive about the other person before leaving.

Review the steps from page 97.

CONFLICT RESOLUTION

RELATE

Have each party declare the resentment to the other party. This must be done without interrogation or interruption. The leader mediates the rules and negotiates the turns.

REQUEST

Have each person state what is desired from the other person in the outcome. Make expectations specific and clear.

RECOGNIZE

Have each person recognize and relate back to the other person an understanding of the request and make an agreement about what part will be honored.

RELATE

Have each person share a positive response to the other before leaving.

REPEAT

When necessary

TEAM BUILDING ROLES

(Grades 9-Adult/Ages 14 and up)

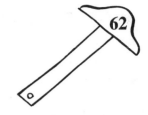

Objective:

To provide an opportunity to experience various role models which often emerge in a group (This group can be a family, participant, staff, leadership or counseling group.)

To increase insight as to models played by the member and define ways to deal with models played by other members

Materials:

☐ Chalkboard and chalk or flipchart and marker

Procedure:

Draw the grid (see right) on the chalkboard or flipchart.

Divide the participants into groups of three with their chairs arranged so that the group members are facing each other. Begin with a warm-up exercise so the group will reach a comfort level.

Begin the exercise by assigning each person in the group an identification letter—A, B, or C. Then explain the grid and the meaning of each role.

ROUND	1	2	3	4
A	3	1	4	2
B	2	4	3	1
C	1	3	2	4

Blamer—A person who never takes personal responsibility but always puts the blame on someone and something else.

Placater—A person who gives in easily, is passive and non-assertive. Whatever suits everybody else suits this person.

Computer—A person who absorbs the data and makes logical decisions. This person wants no funny business and is very serious.

Digresser—A person who seems unable to keep on task. This person always has something else to talk about and continually interrupts the group with his/her own agenda.

Assign the roles they will play, blamer (1), placater (2), computer (3), or digresser (4). Each role will be assigned to a letter. According to the grid in the first round, for example, the group member designated A will play the role of the computer, B the placater, and C the blamer. One role, the digresser, is rotated so that observations can be made as to the addition or deletion of that role.

After assigning the roles for the first round, select a topic and give the participants about three minutes to discuss the topic, adhering strictly to their assigned roles. Then reassign the roles. According to the grid in the second round, for example, the group member designated A will now play the role of the Blamer, B the Digresser, and C the Computer. Use the same topic so that comparisons can be made of the role response. Continue to shift the roles group members role-play according to the grid until at least four rounds have been completed.

When four or more rounds have been completed, instruct participants to move into a large circle and discuss what happened. Use lead questions such as:

- "What did you see happening to communication in your group?"
- "Who took the lead in making something happen?"
- "Who was the hardest to work with?"
- "Who seemed indispensable?"
- "Who would you most like to do without?"
- "Which role do you, personally, find yourself playing?"

Next, ask the participants for ideas about improving communication in their everyday lives. Then choose a topic of immediate concern for discussion.

For example:

- Where shall we eat lunch today?
- Where shall we hold the class (staff) picnic?

Note: Although this exercise has been used by many leaders, the originator was Virginia Satir.

JUMPING HURDLES

(Grades 4-12/Ages 9-18)

Objective:

To learn to identify barriers and problem solve a way to jump over hurdles

Materials:

☐ Overhead transparency and marker or chalkboard and chalk
☐ Paper and a pencil for each participant

Procedure:

Make an overhead transparency or draw a picture on the chalkboard of the hurdle (see right). Distribute a piece of paper and a pencil to each participant. Show the group members the sample hurdle and instruct them to draw a picture of a hurdle like one on the transparency/chalkboard. On the line above *My Goal,* instruct the participants to write something they have always wanted to do but haven't been able to do, or something that they would like to do better. On the crossbar of the hurdle, tell the participants to write the things that seem to keep them from reaching this goal or doing what they want to do.

On left side of the paper, have the participants write all of the strengths they have which would enable them to accomplish their goal. On the right side of the paper, the participants should write the limitations which might keep them from accomplishing their goal. Down the middle of the paper have them write the "outside forces" which might be in their way. Now have them review the barriers and put an ✗ by the ones over which they have no control. Draw a circle around the "outside forces" over which they do have some control. Then have the participants decide on three things they can do to overcome the barriers.

Break the participants into groups of five and have the group members help each other think of ways to overcome the barriers. Conclude the lesson by having each person write on the back of his/her paper a plan for reaching the thing he/she has always wanted to do and set a time to start on the plan.

Note: The leader may want to demonstrate the problem-solving model on page 93 before giving this assignment.

ATTITUDES TOWARD AUTHORITY

(Adults)

Objective:

To assist participants in identifying their leadership style and understanding how it affects their subordinates (This can be used with participants, teachers, or in leader/follower relationships where clarification of style can improve performance.)

Materials:

- ☐ Chalkboard and chalk
- ☐ Paper and a pencil for each participant

Procedure:

This activity can elicit very strong emotional responses from participants and some rapport in the group needs to be built before doing the exercise. Before introducing this exercise, be sure you are comfortable with your own authority T—square results and in your competence in leading groups of adults. Since this activity can evoke deep feelings in the participants, the leader needs to be prepared to respond with appropriate responses. Group members need to be told that the activity explores their relationship with their earliest authority figure and that influence on their present authority role. Be sure that they are not pressed to share any findings. They must know, as in all groups, that it is permissible not to participate.

Use an icebreaker to prepare the group for the exercise. You can find some ideas in the section *Tools for Starting Groups* (pages 15-20) of this book, which would be light and appropriate. Distribute a piece of paper and a pencil to each participant. The proceed with the following steps:

1. Give an overview of the theory behind the activity by saying:

    The ATTITUDE TOWARD AUTHORITY is based on the transactional analysis model. TA was developed by Eric Berne and has been popularized by the writings of Tom Harris, "I'm OK, You're OK," Jongeward, James, and the Gouldings. "TA is an interactional therapy grounded on the assumption that we make current decisions based on past premises that were once appropriate to our survival needs but may no longer be valid. It stresses that the person can change and make new decisions different from the rules and regulations they learned as children." (Theory and Practice of Group Counseling. Gerald Corey, Page 311.)

2. Have the participants draw a T-square on a piece of paper. Demonstrate on the chalkboard or paper how to make it. On the top of the T-square, they should write the name of the one person who was the most powerful figure for them before age 10. If it is difficult to choose between parents, choose the stronger one and use the

other parent later. The choice may be a grandparent or even a neighbor depending on the makeup of the family. On the left side of the T-square, write a description of that person. On the right side of the T-square, write your responses to that person and your feelings as a child. It is important to try to look back at the feelings you had then—not the feelings you have now.

3. Ask the participants to list three positive qualities which they admired in this person on the left side of the T-square below their description of the person. Give some examples. You may add that even if you hated this person, try to find something good. Now move to the right side and write your feelings as a child about those positive qualities. For example, that person may have been so wonderful that you always felt that you couldn't achieve that same perfection, or he/she may have been so terrible that you always felt superior. As a child, you may have always felt protected. Get in touch with those feelings.

4. Ask the participants to list three negative qualities which they did not like about this person on the left side of the T-square below the list of positive qualities. It may be difficult to think of any negatives if you always admired the person. Maybe you have thought the person was perfect. That in itself may have been a negative. Now move to the right side of the T-square and tell how that made you feel as a child. Give some examples of feelings which might have been experienced.

5. Ask the participants to write three adjectives on the left side of the T-square which they would use to describe the person. These may be somewhat repetitious of the first two descriptions or it may be a combination of the positive and negative. Now move to the right side and describe your childhood feelings about what you wrote.

6. If you were sick or injured or down emotionally, how would that person have reacted? Give examples—would he/she have been loving and nurturing or would he/she have ignored the crises and indicated that you must "get on with it." Write your answers on the left side of the T-square. Now move to the right side and describe your childhood feelings as they relate to the examples.

7. Write the message you received as a child about your worthwhileness on the left side of the T-square. (This may need to be explained.) Was this person saying that you were important or that you were in the way? Did you absorb more non-verbally than verbally? Now move to the right side and describe your childhood feelings as they relate to your worthwhileness.

8. Write the recurring message that you still receive from that person about your worthwhileness on the left side of the T-square. It doesn't matter the age of the person now or even whether that person is still living. You probably still get a message. Now move to the right side and describe your feelings now.

9. Allow some silent time for the participants to process the above information. During this period of silence, ask them to look at the total information which has

been brought into their awareness. Then give them time to share with the group any discoveries which they have made about their authority person and their relationship to that person. *Caution:* Some memories may have surfaced which had been long buried. It is possible that someone will discover a happy concept which can be shared with the group. It is not unusual for someone to be touched to the point of tears when reaching back to such memories. Sometimes, for those with a very neglected or harsh childhood, the discovery that they were alone in the group is devastating. Handle these moments gently without probing deeply.

10. Guide the sharing with the following questions. Allow members to volunteer to participate. Do not have each person share around the circle. You may be touching on ground too sensitive for group confrontation.

   A. In what way do I express my authority role like the person I just described? What traits do I communicate to others who are my subordinates? children? participants?

   B. In what way do I respond to the persons in authority over me in the same way I respond to the person chosen.

   C. In view of my past, what are my expectations and needs from people in authority?

   D. In what ways would I like to change the way I express my authority role in relation to my subordinates?

   E. In what ways would I like to change the way I respond to persons in authority over me?

   F. In what ways do I operate or live my life according to the way I reacted or felt as child?

   G. In what ways do I operate or live my life in exactly the opposite manner from the way I felt and reacted as a child?

   H. In what way does my present behavior reflect the those feelings?

Conclude the exercise by having the participants complete the following:

From this exercise

- I have learned …
- I have relearned …
- I have realized …
- I am surprised that …

ROLE-PLAY

(Grades 2-Adult/Ages 7 and up)

Objective:

To demonstrate the potential of role-playing when clarification of a situation is needed

Materials:

None.

Procedure:

When a person is playing the "blaming" game or is upset with a peer, teacher, or parent, listen to him/her, then ask the him/her to enact the role of the person in conflict.

You might say:

"In order for us to better understand what is happening here, I would like you to let me play the role of you and you be the other person involved. You assume the role of your friend, tell me how you see and feel the situation, and I'll try to respond as I think you would. We may role-play several different ways to see if we can discover one that will help the situation."

Younger or shy children may need a little help in starting the role-play. Another alternative is to have the participants write out both roles until they find a satisfactory solutions.

This activity can result in:

- Better insight into another person's point of view.

- Clearer understanding of the other person's feelings.

- More objective understanding of your own responses.

- Opening of more negotiating opportunities.

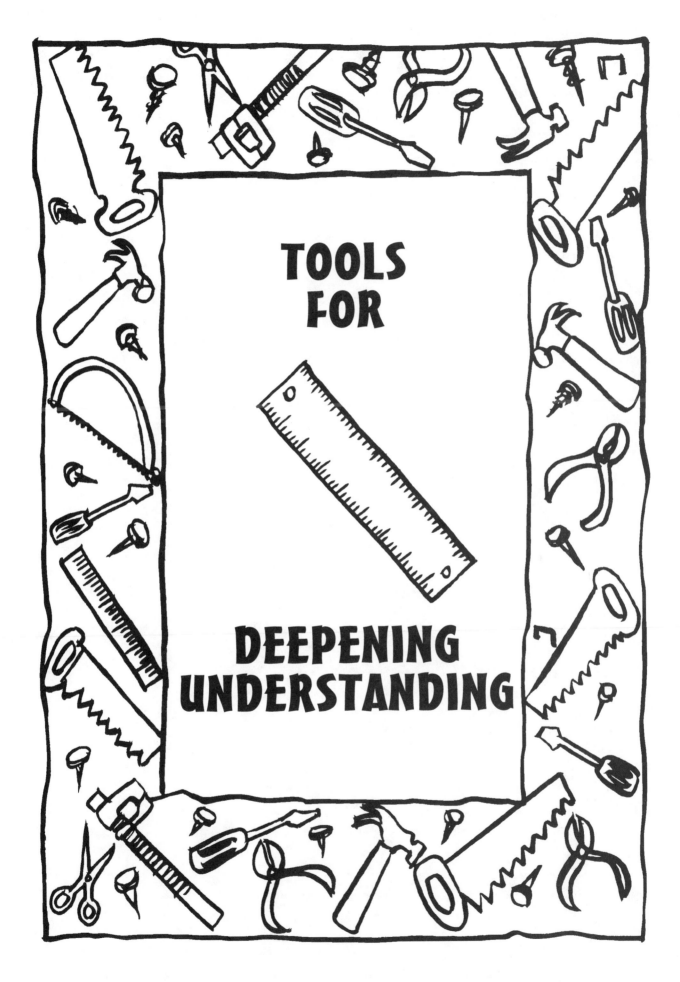

TOOLS
FOR

DEEPENING
UNDERSTANDING

OPEN-ENDED SENTENCES

(Grades 1-12/Ages 6-18)

Objective:

To encourage participants to deal with feelings by helping them identify and express deeper emotions and gain understanding

Materials:

☐ List of incomplete sentences (see below)

Procedure:

This activity can be used as a break from academic work, as a relaxer, or as a teacher in the affective domain. Time needs to be planned for a good discussion or a way of processing what has happened in the group. It can be used in a total classroom setting or in small groups.

Ask the participants to sit in a circle. Read one open-ended sentence and have each group member who chooses to complete the sentence. If someone does not want to participate all he/she has to do is say "I pass." Continue this process until all the sentences have been read or the allotted time has elapsed. You may add additional questions to the list.

1. Tests make me feel _____ .
2. I would like to have _____ .
3. It bothers me when _____ .
4. After school, I like to _____ .
5. At home in the evening, I usually _____ .
6. My most special possession is _____ .
7. Our family likes to _____ .
8. I am afraid of _____ .
9. My favorite television program is _____ .
10. When I am very good, my parents let me _____ .
11. Something I like that belongs to me is _____ .
12. My favorite activity at school is _____ .

All of the open-ended sentences may not elicit answers which express feelings. A way to extend the participant's response is to add "How does that make you feel?"

FRIENDSHIP

(Grades 4-Adult/Ages 9 and up)

Objective:

To help clarify the fragility of relationships and the value of friendship

To assist participants in understanding the feelings associated with the loss of a friend

Materials:

☐ 4" x 4" piece of paper for each participant

Procedure:

Distribute a 4" x 4" piece of paper to each participant. Ask the group members to visualize the paper as the one person that they love most in their lives. Remain in silence until they have had time to develop this image. Guide their thinking by having them look at the paper and visualize the following:

- The appearance of the person
- Acts of kindness by the person
- Special shared activities with the person
- Any other ties which bind them to that individual

Next, tell the participants that you want them to destroy the paper by tearing it up. Wait in silence until this has been done. Now ask them to put the paper back together in its original form. Since they will probably be unsuccessful at reconstructing the paper, give them time to process this experience and the accompanying feelings. If they are not mentioned, discuss the following truths:

- When we hurt someone, it is nearly impossible to repair.
- When we lose friendship, it is hard to grieve the loss.
- When we have pleasant memories, they are hard to give up.

Have the group continue to reveal thoughts and feelings for as long as time allows.

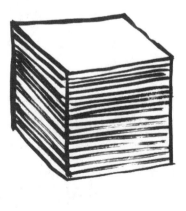

PROMOTE FRIENDSHIP

(Grades K-8/Ages 5-13)

Objective:

To teach participants some gestures of friendship which will promote cooperation, awareness of others and the concept of kindness

Materials:

☐ See each individual suggestion for materials required

Procedure:

1. Make a group booklet writing and illustrating responses to "What Is A Friend?" or "How Do I Choose A Friend?"

2. Plan an activity in which each participant makes something for a friend as a demonstration of affection. Discuss the difference between making something and buying something.

3. Train several children to run a "Welcoming Station" as a way of introducing new participants to the class/group. Appoint a committee to run the station at certain times and to make decisions about how to run the station.

4. Make individual booklets about friends. List specific friends. Include such pages as:

   - Friends that are girls.
   - Friends that are boys.
   - Friends that are animals.
   - Friends that are grown-ups.

5. Develop a friendship corner where participants who are having disagreements can go to settle their problems. When the problem is resolved, they may rejoin the class. (See Tool 61, page 96 on conflict resolution for additional information.)

6. Organize a "Secret Pal Program" for a week or more. Members should do some nice things for their secret pals which do not cost money.

7. Have "Special Conference Times" in which some group leaders meet with specific students for about 10-15 minutes to participate in friendly conversation. This can teach conversational skills.

8. Gather together some books about friendship. Leave them in a friendship corner. Have them available for reading at special relaxation times. Lead short discussions about their content.

FRIENDSHIP BANNER

(Grades 4-8/Ages 9-13)

Objective:

To provide participants an opportunity to increase their awareness of the qualities of good friendship

Materials:

☐ Picture of a large banner with space for decorating with symbols and a pencil or crayons for each participant

Procedure:

Lead a short discussion on the meaning of friendship. Distribute a picture of a large banner and a pencil or crayons to each participant. Instruct them to decorate their banners with symbols which represent the following:

- something you look for when choosing a friend
- something about you that makes you a good friend
- something you would like to give a friend
- something you would like a friend to give you
- how you felt when someone was friendly to you

Have the participants share their banners with the group and interpret the meaning of their symbols. Conclude the activity with a review of the meaning of friendship.

WATER FANTASY

(Grades 4-Adult/Ages 9 and up)

Objective:

To provide a structure for deepening relationships (This activity is most effective after the group has had some time together to get acquainted.)

Materials:

None.

Procedure:

Divide the participants into groups of four. Tell each person to think of him/herself as a form of water. The participants should choose the form of water that would best describe their personalities, tell where the water would be located, and why they chose it.

Examples of forms of water:

- Mist on a leaf
- Ice on a frozen lake
- A swimming pool in a park
- A waterfall
- A mountain stream
- An ocean
- A river
- A glass of spring water
- A pond on a farm
- A tidal wave

Alternative fantasies to use with a group:

- Animal fantasy
- Sound fantasy
- Window fantasy
- Flower fantasy
- Color fantasy
- Transportation fantasy (train, tricycle, jet, etc.)
- Book fantasy
- Clothing fantasy

It is important to process the insights gained from this experience. Input from group members about what they see in each other can be helpful.

OPINION
(Grades 9-Adult/Ages 14 and up)

Objective:

To deepen relationships and to stimulate the ability to think together in a compatible manner

Materials:

☐ List of words to stimulate a generalized discussion (see suggestions below)

Procedure:

Before using this tool, establish some rapport and understanding in the group by using some of the starter activities in this book (pages 15-20). Explain the importance of acceptance of differences and recognition of those early influences on our current positions.

Present a generalized subject such as "money" as a topic for discussion. Ask the group members to describe their perception of this subject and its value during their childhood—prior to age 10. When the selected subject has been described, ask them to describe their current beliefs or values related to the subject.

Example:
Describe the importance of money and your attitudes toward money in your childhood prior to age 10. Include the effects money had on your attitude and development.

Participant:
Money was very important to us as children since we were poor and never had enough. I can remember saving an ice cream cone because I was afraid I would never get another one, and being afraid that the electricity man would come cut the power off because my dad hadn't paid the bill.

Participant (second round):
Money is important to me now because I am a careful saver. I am careful about spending, just as I was careful to save the ice cream cone. It seems that I want to be sure that I don't run out of money.

Ideas for generalized subjects may be:

Money	Authority	Education	Charity
Freedom	Politics	Prejudice	War
Family	Religion	Involvement	

The leader may choose any subjects which seem relevant to the group situation. Some of these may be too controversial to give participants a comfortable sharing experience. However, if good rapport and community has been established, it may give participants experience in hearing and accepting the right of another person to have opinions different from their own.

A GESTALT ACTIVITY

(Grades 4-Adult/Ages 9 and up)

Objective:

To project a self-image to use for interpretation and to become more self-aware

Materials:

☐ Basket or paper bag; collection of small items from a purse or desk such as a marker, a paper clip, a pin, scotch tape, a coin, a small book, a calender, a cassette tape, a video tape, etc.

Procedure:

Drop the articles in the basket or paper bag. Hold the basket/bag so the participants can draw one item without seeing it. When each person has an item, give the following instructions:

> "You now have your own specific item. I would like you to fantasize that you are that item and describe yourself. For example, you could say, 'I am a paper clip. I am made of metal and easily bent.'"

Each person then takes a turn describing him/herself in terms of the item. When every person has given his/her description, explain that there may be a relationship between what they said about the item and what they would say about themselves. Ask the group members to voluntarily reveal anything they have learned about that relationship. For example: "I'm like the paper clip because I would rather bend and get along than argue and take a chance on losing a friend."

This activity can create deep feelings. Handle with care any threatening revelation which may be too much for the participant to deal with in the group setting.

PROJECTION

(Grades 3-Adult/Ages 8 and up)

Objective:

To increase participants' self-understanding

Materials:

None.

Procedure:

Ask the participants to imagine that they are a different person or thing (see suggestions below). Then tell the participants to think about how they would see the world in a new way if they were this person or thing.

Examples:

- Giant
- Bug
- Bird
- Trapeze artist

Examples to personalize this activity:

- Parent
- Teacher
- Grandparent

You can also have participants dramatize the identified issue using role-play.

Examples:

- Parents who are too strict.
- Teachers who give too much homework.
- Grandparent who comes to visit.

This activity will help participants see the world through someone else's eyes.

LOOKING BACK

(Grades 5-Adult/Ages 10 and up)

Objective:

To increase participants' awareness of life values

Materials:

- ☐ Copy of activity sheet (see below) and a pencil for each participant
- ☐ Chalkboard and chalk or flipchart and marker

Procedure:

Distribute a copy of the activity sheet and a pencil to each participant. Then instruct the group members to write answers to the following question:

"If I was 85 years of age and looking back at my life, what five things would I want to be able to say about it?"

Give the group members adequate time to think about the question and to write their answers. When each member of the group has finished writing, ask for volunteers to share one or two of their thoughts. Write some of the responses on a chalkboard or flipchart. Then ask:

"What does this mean to our lives now and in the near future?"

This can be a good lead-in exercise to precede a goal-setting activity.

NAME _____

> **"If I was 85 years of age and looking back at my life, what five things would I want to be able to say about it?**

1. _____

2. _____

3. _____

4. _____

5. _____

INSIDE/OUTSIDE

(Grades 4-Adult/Ages 9 and up)

Objective:

To learn to distinguish between the inner self and the outer self by becoming more self-aware.

Materials:

☐ Small paper bag, gluestick, magazines, scissors, and magic markers for each participant

Procedure:

Tell the group:

"This activity focuses on thinking about yourself, how you look, what you like, and how you feel."

Distribute a small paper bag, a gluestick, magazines, scissors, and magic markers to each participant. Then give the following explanation to the group:

1. On the outside of the bag, cut out and glue pictures or words that tell about your outside self—the self that everybody sees and knows. You may write words or glue pictures to indicate what you think others see.

2. On the inside of the bag, cut out and place pictures or words about your inner self— the secret self that you know but most people do not know. This will involve how you feel.

3. When you have completed both the inside and the outside of the bag, decide what you want to do with your bag. You may share the outside with someone else, you may share the inside with someone else, or you may be willing to share both sides. There may be things you do not want to share with anyone. There may be things you want to share, but are uncomfortable doing so.

4. As you make your decisions, we will divide into small groups of four where you may choose what you would like to share.

Be sure the group understands that any person is free not to share if he/she chooses. Do not rush this exercise. You may extend the exercise over more than one session.

MYSELF/YOURSELF

(Grades K-4/Ages 5-9)

Objective:

To increase participants' awareness of self and others

To learn to verbalize self-awareness

Materials:

☐ Mural paper, scissors, magazines, gluestick, and a marker for each participant

Procedure:

Distribute a sheet of mural paper, scissors, magazines, a gluestick, and a marker to each participant. Divide the group members into pairs. Have one person lie on the mural paper while the partner traces his/her outline with a marker. Repeat this procedure having the partners exchange roles. Then tell the participants to cut out pictures or words from magazines and glue them on the silhouette to make a collage that will describe what they are like, things they think about, and things they feel. Then instruct the participants to cut out their silhouettes.

Post the collages on a bulletin board or around the room. Give the participants time to share details about themselves by describing the reasoning behind their selections on their collages.

Alternative:

Reverse the exercise and let the participants make a collage about someone else in the group. Use the same procedure. This exercise can increase participants' awareness of other people. Be sure that they understand that no insults or put-downs are to be used on the collages.

SHARE A QUOTE
(Grades 6-Adult/Ages 11 and up)

77

Objective:

To promote a deeper level of group participation and encourage group members to take some responsibility in contributing to the group

Materials:

☐ Copy of the quotes (see below) for each participant (optional)

Procedure:

Before the session, either ask the group members to bring a quote or saying which has had a impact on their lives to the next meeting, give them a copy of the quotes below, or use some personal favorites. It does not matter if the leader understands the author's meaning. What is important is the interpretation by the individual group member.

Divide the participants into small groups. Have each participant share the quote he/she chose with the group and explain why it is significant to him/her. Invite responses from the other group members as feedback.

"We find in life exactly what we put into it "
> Ralph Waldo Emerson

"Perhaps the most important single cause of a person's success or failure has to do with the question of what he believes about himself."
> Arther W. Combs

"I can trust my own experience—evaluation by others is not a guide for me."
> Carl Rogers

"The problems of the world essentially are the problems of individuals. If individuals can change, the course of the world can change. This is a hope worth sustaining."
> Tom Harris

"School is a battleground for too many participants, a place where major confrontations and minor skirmishes occur daily."
> Richard L. Curwin

"Things turn out best for people who make the best out of the ways things turn out."
> Art Linkletter

LEARNING CHECK UP

(Grades 4-12/Ages 9-18)

Objective:

To review and bring closure to the last session of a group or workshop by having participants reflect on their experiences

Materials:

☐ Copy of *Learning Checkup* and a pencil for each participant
☐ Laminated list or poster of the following statements:
  - I learned or relearned _____ .
  - I realized _____ .
  - I was surprised by _____ .
  - I discovered that _____ .

Procedure:

Show the list/poster to the participants. Explain that this is an evaluation sheet for both yourself and them. Distribute a copy of *Learning Checkup* and a pencil to each person. Tell the participants how much time they have to complete the sheet. When the allotted time has elapsed, ask them to share at least one statement from their activity sheets. Collect the sheets to read and review at a later time.

LEARNING CHECK UP

NAME _____

I learned or relearned _____

_____

_____ .

I realized _____

_____

_____ .

I was surprised by _____

_____

_____ .

I discovered that _____

_____

_____ .

HOUSEHOLD

(Grades 5-Adult/Ages 10 and up)

Objective:

To encourage participants' identification with life periods and the influence of feelings in each period

Materials:

☐ Paper and crayons or colored pencils for each participant

Procedure:

Distribute a piece of paper and crayons or colored pencils to each participant. Instruct the group members to divide their papers into four equal parts by drawing lines or folding the paper. In each quadrant, ask the group members to draw a house or surroundings which represent four different periods of their lives, using colors which represent their feelings about that period. When the group members have finished drawing, ask them to share information about the situation and the feelings which they were experiencing at the four time periods represented and feelings which they have currently.

INDIVIDUALITY COOKIE

(Grades 2-Adult/Ages 7 and up)

Objective:

To assist participants in identifying and understanding the value of their uniqueness

Materials:

☐ Plate for each small group
☐ Chocolate chip cookie or other object which has a definite individuality for each participant

Procedure:

Give each group member one cookie. Explain that this will be their special cookie, so they need to remember every detail about it. Tell the group members to observe the size of the cookie, the location of the chips, and any unique patterns about the arrangement of the chips on the cookie. Tell the participants how much time they have to complete this part of the activity.

When the allotted time has elapsed, divide the participants into groups of approximately six members. Instruct the group members to randomly place their cookies on the plate. (The cookies should be well mixed.) Ask each person to find his/her own cookie by looking for the characteristics he/she previously observed and remove the cookie from the plate. No one should take another person's cookie. If a group member is uncertain as to which cookie belongs to him/her, he/she may pass. If anyone disagrees with someone else about ownership, that person must explain why he/she thinks the cookie is his/hers. After everyone has had a turn, those group members who passed or guessed incorrectly may take another turn.

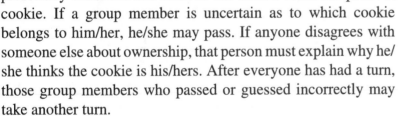

After all the cookies have been selected, lead a discussion about the individuality of the cookies as compared with the participants own uniqueness. Discuss individual differences and likenesses. Help each member to identify something that makes him/her unique, special and different from the other members of the group.

OPEN-ENDED EXCHANGE

(Grades 4-Adult/Ages 9 and up)

Objective:

To provide participants with a success experience, promote positive self-concept, and develop involvement, thinking, and communication skills

To teach participants respectful interaction and increase cohesiveness

Materials:

None.

Procedure:

This exercise is especially effective because it requires no preliminary preparation and provides a non-judgmental atmosphere of trust and learning. It is excellent preparation for a learning experience and can be used effectively as an opener to promote a receptive atmosphere.

Instruct the group to form a tight circle with no obstructions in the center. The leader should also have a place in the circle and change places each time the group meets. Explain to the group members that they will have a specific amount of time to discuss a topic which you will give them. The length of the discussion will vary according to the maturity of the participants. Holding the discussions to a specific time limit increases the participants sense of responsibility and provides an atmosphere of security. Hand raising, although orderly at the beginning, will soon be unnecessary as participants understand the expectations.

Tell the participants the following:

- One person talks at a time.
- Everyone's opinion will be respected.
- An opinion can be challenged if done constructively.
- No put-downs will be tolerated.

The leader should always provide support through direction. This is done by creating an atmosphere of warmth and enthusiasm through body language, voice tone, and willingness to be a responsive listener. The art of questioning is very important, and more effective leaders refrain from repeating and rephrasing answers, limit "teacher-talk" whenever possible, and do not moralize.

Make a list of some open-ended ideas which can be used as discussion starters. Include a definition, an interpretation of the meaning of the word used, and a personalization of that meaning.

For example:

- What is mud?
- How can mud be used?
- What can you do with mud?

This is a simple approach which will lead to participation by everybody. No knowledge is needed and there is little chance to be wrong if only words which lend themselves to generalities are used.

Ideas for beginning definitions:

- What is a cloud?
- What is a radio?
- What is a rock?
- What is a mountain?
- What is a lake?
- What is an attitude?
- What is appreciation?
- What is cooperation?
- What is integrity?
- What is patriotism?
- What is a school?
- What is an institution?
- What is a feeling?
- What is anger?
- What is hostility?
- What is kindness?
- What is politeness?
- What is love?

This list is inexhaustible. At the end evaluate by processing the experience using the question, "What have we learned from the experience." Note—This was originally called a Class Meeting and was used and experienced by the trainers from the Glasser Training Center.

Following the session the leader should ask him/herself the following questions:

- What satisfied me most about this experience?
- Did any especially positive occurrences happen?
- How did I encourage an increase of involvement and thinking?
- Is there anything I would do differently?
- What future class discussion topics did this meeting suggest?

TURNING POINTS

(Grades 5-Adult/Ages 10 and up)

Objective:

To encourage participants to identify significant events in their lives and how they relate to present attitudes

Materials:

☐ Paper and a pencil for each participant

Procedure:

Distribute a piece of paper and a pencil to each participant. Instruct the participants to draw a straight line across the bottom of their papers. Explain that this line represents their life line and they are to assume that the line starts with birth and goes to this moment. Have each participant draw four dots on the line to represent times when his/her life-style and/or values changed, then beneath each dot write his/her age at that point and over the dot write the change that occurred at that age.

For example:

- Start of school
- Parents divorced
- Arrival of a new baby
- Theft of an important object
- Older sibling leaves home
- Moved to a new city
- Grandmother's death
- Family member is very ill
- Facing a personal illness
- Father lost job

If the group is small, together discuss the effects these turning points had on their lives and what they are thinking or doing currently. If the group is too large, divide the group members into triads or dyads, and have each group hold its own discussion.

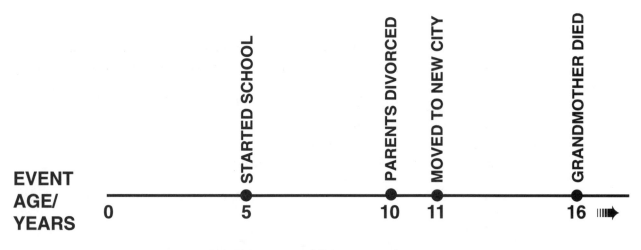

LIKENESSES AND DIFFERENCES

(Grades 4-12/Ages 9-18)

Objective:

To encourage participants to observe and accept the fact that all persons have likenesses and differences

To increase participants' observational skills

Materials:

☐ Chalkboard and chalk or flipchart and marker, one-minute timer
☐ Paper and a pencil for each participant

Procedure:

This exercise is good to use in working with racial prejudices and prejudices against handicaps. Distribute a piece of paper and a pencil to each participant. Choose six individuals with differences in appearances to stand up in front of the group. Instruct the group members to observe each person carefully for one minute without speaking. During this observation, ask them to jot down on a piece of paper any differences they observe. (Make a rule which will assure that no derogatory remarks are made.)

For example:

- Some are tall and some are short.
- Some have blond hair and some have dark hair.
- Some are girls and some are boys.
- Some have light skin and some have dark skin.

Then give the group members another minute to observe the individuals likenesses and to jot them down. Discuss each of these observations with the entire group, making a list of differences and likenesses on a chalkboard/flipchart.

When the list is completed, discuss the observations in terms of the ways they affect our acceptance of each other and our getting along with each other. Stimulate the discussion by asking the following questions:

- How important are these differences?
- Do these differences change our relationships?
- Is it necessary to have likenesses to form relationships?

PREJUDICE

(Grades 4-12/Ages 9-18)

Objective:

To identify areas of prejudice, ways to respond to prejudice, and ways to overcome prejudice

Materials:

☐ Paper and a pencil for each participant

Procedure:

Select five group members who have special differences. Be sure to contact them ahead of time to ask their willingness to participate in this exercise. Another approach is to ask for volunteers from the group. State: "For this exercise, I need the help of five people who have some differences which may or may not be obvious." Have each of the five participants describe his/her difference in one sentence.

For example:

- I am Hispanic.
- I am Cuban.
- I am African-American.
- I am from Iraq.
- I am Jewish.
- My father was in prison.
- I come from a single-parent family.
- I am a latch-key kid.
- My parents never went to college.
- My parents have doctoral degrees.
- I can't read.
- I am in special education.

As each person speaks, have the group members write the first five descriptive responses they think of about the person.

For example: I am a latch-key kid. Five impressions:

- Neglected
- Lonely
- Single-parent
- Undisciplined
- Too much responsibility

When the everyone has finished writing their impressions for all five volunteers, have them share their impressions with the group and elicit responses from the individuals involved. Discuss the causes of prejudices, the harm done, and ways to break down the walls of misunderstanding.

COOPERATIVE POSTER

(Grades 6-Adult/Ages 11 and up)

Objective:

To teach participants group cooperation and team building

Materials:

☐ Table, magazines, gluesticks, magic markers of various colors, scissors, and clock
☐ Piece of tag board for each group

Procedure:

Place all the materials on one table so the group members will have to organize a method for obtaining them. Be sure to have available fewer pairs of scissors and gluesticks than there are groups. This provides the necessity of learning to cooperate with other groups to obtain available materials.

Divide the participants into groups of six to eight members. Spread out so that a working area is available for each group. Introduce the topic of leadership (any other subject can be used with this same method) and team cooperation. Instruct each group to make a poster illustrating good leadership and team building out of the materials available. Allow at least 30-60 minutes for this activity. Warn the groups at time intervals about how much time is left.

When the posters are complete, ask each group to appoint a clean-up crew. Then have them display their posters in a specified place with one member appointed by his/her group to explain the poster. After all the posters have been presented, have the entire group vote on the best poster by rounds of applause. Select a winner. This may be hard to do since each group is likely to support its own poster. The message is, "We support what we help to produce."

Conclude the activity by asking the following:

- What did you see happening in your group that made a cooperative team?
- What did you see happening in your group that blocked production?
- Who did you see emerging as the leader?
- How does this activity fit into a workshop on leadership?
- How does this experience relate to what you do in your work (classroom, business, club, school, sports, church, etc.)

VALUES PIE

(Grades 6-Adult/Ages 11 and up)

Objective:

To help participants prioritize their values and define their goals

Materials:

- ☐ Chalkboard and chalk or flipchart and marker
- ☐ Copy of a large circle on a piece of paper and a pencil for each participant

Procedure:

Write the word list (see below) and draw a sample pie chart on the chalkboard/flipchart. Read the list of topics aloud to the group and show them the sample pie chart. Explain what a pie chart is and how this sample depicts how one person might rate the important things in his/her life. Then tell the participants to choose the things which they believe are the most important in their lives. Instruct them to divide their circle proportionately in slices like a pie, giving the things of highest value the largest piece of their pie.

Sample Word List:

- Health
- Intelligence
- Achievement
- Family
- Kindness
- Romance
- Honesty
- Education
- Money
- Good Looks
- Fame
- Career
- Influence
- Travel
- Reputation
- Position

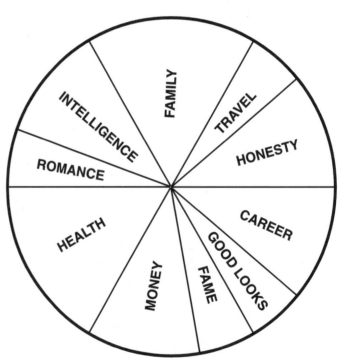

When the participants have completed their pie charts, ask them to share their charts with the group, discuss what influenced their choices, and what effect those choices could have on future decisions.

JOURNAL KEEPING

(Grades 4-Adult/Ages 9 and up)

Objective:

To provide a way for participants to record their feelings and impressions daily or at the time of a traumatic experience (This is an excellent therapeutic tool for releasing feelings.)

Materials:

☐ Notebook (preferably spiral) for each person keeping a journal

Procedure:

Journal writing may be done in or outside the group situation. If journals are to be kept in the room where the group meets, they must be stored in a locked place to ensure the writers' privacy. The information in each journal is very personal and should not be shared without the permission of the writer. Journal writing in the classroom can be a nice relaxation exercise.

Tell the participants:

"One of the ways you may find satisfying in expressing your real feelings is keeping a journal. It is very similar to keeping a diary, except that you are more concerned about recording feelings than facts. Use a ring bound or loose leaf notebook and keep it in a private place. Write in it every time you find yourself thinking about something dealing with your feelings. It is not necessary to write everyday, but you will find that setting a regular time will be most helpful. It is not necessary to reread your writings unless you find comfort in looking back at your feelings and enjoying the progress you have made. Sometimes on bad days, it is good to read about the good days."

Journal keeping is a way to:

- Grow as a person
- Sort out conflicts
- Clarify issues
- Establish new goals
- Track trends in feelings and behavior
- Take more control of your life

You may find comfort in:

- Writing a letter to someone
- Writing out your questions
- Expressing your anger directly
- Writing about something you have lost
- Writing out your dreams
- Writing about the pain on the printed page

When you are journal writing, leave it exactly as you write it. Do not give thought to grammatical errors, corrections, or ways of expression. Be spontaneous! Let the thoughts and feelings flow naturally. Never go back to correct, change, mark out, or defend what you wrote.

LITTLE THINGS ABOUT ME

(Grades 6-Adult/Ages 11 and up)

Objective:

To provide an opportunity for a person to gain more self awareness, to share this awareness with a group, and enable the group to share acceptance of each other

Materials:

☐ Copy of *Little Things About Me* (see below) and a pencil for each participant

Procedure:

Distribute a copy of *Little Things About Me* and a pencil to each participant. Instruct the participants to complete the form. When everyone has finished, allow time for the group members to share information about themselves with at least one other person or the whole group. This is a very non-threatening method of getting people to share something about themselves.

LITTLE THINGS ABOUT ME
by

_____

Things I love   _____   _____

                                                  _____   _____

Things I hate   _____   _____

  _____   _____

Things I enjoy   _____   _____

  _____   _____

Things I cherish   _____   _____

  _____   _____

Things I want   _____   _____

  _____   _____

Things I miss   _____   _____

  _____   _____

ALL ABOUT ME
(Grades 5-12/Ages 10-18)

Objective:

To increase participants' self-awareness through examining cognitive material

Materials:

☐ Copy of *All About Me* (pages 132-133) and a pencil for each participant

Procedure:

Explain the importance of becoming more self-aware in the process of developing self-understanding and personal growth.

State the following:

"Fritz Perls, a famous psychiatrist, has told us 'everything starts in awareness.' Today we are going to do some work to increase our self-awareness and examine our image of ourselves. (Distribute a copy of *All About Me* and a pencil to each participant.) Read each topic carefully and check all the boxes which you think apply to you. Do this as accurately as you can. Remember that you do not have to share your answers unless you wish to do so."

After the form is completed, encourage participation in sharing discoveries by asking the following questions:

- What did you mark on the chart that you felt sure about?

- What did you discover that surprised you?

- What did you experience that you were unsure of?

- What perceptions of yourself would you like validation for from other members?

- What are some things you cannot change?

- What is your plan for making some of those changes?

- What have you learned from this experience which can influence the way you do things?

This is a good time to introduce goal-setting for the next group session.

ALL ABOUT ME

MY PHYSICAL SELF

I see myself as:
- [ ] tall
- [ ] middle sized
- [ ] short
- [ ] fat
- [ ] average weight
- [ ] thin
- [ ] strong
- [ ] medium strength
- [ ] weak
- [ ] very attractive
- [ ] fairly attractive
- [ ] acceptable
- [ ] ugly
- [ ] quite agile
- [ ] coordinated
- [ ] clumsy
- [ ] I like my appearance
- [ ] I would like to improve my appearance
- [ ] I dislike my appearance

Other people:
- [ ] like my appearance
- [ ] don't notice my appearance
- [ ] dislike my appearance
- [ ] make fun of my appearance

Things I can change about my appearance:

_____

_____

Ways I can go about the change:

_____

_____

_____

Things I must accept that I can't change:

_____

_____

_____

MY INTELLECTUAL SELF

I rate myself as:
- [ ] bright
- [ ] reasonably smart
- [ ] average
- [ ] below average
- [ ] slow
- [ ] dumb
- [ ] smarter than most peers
- [ ] equal to most peers
- [ ] slower than most peers
- [ ] good in word activities
- [ ] poor in word activities
- [ ] good in math activities
- [ ] poor in math activities
- [ ] good in thinking activities
- [ ] poor in thinking activities
- [ ] good in creative activities
- [ ] poor in creative activities

I learn best by:
- [ ] writing it down
- [ ] seeing it
- [ ] hearing it
- [ ] doing it
- [ ] repeating it
- [ ] copying it
- [ ] memorizing it

Talents I can develop: _____

_____

_____

My reading skills are:
- [ ] very comfortable
- [ ] weak
- [ ] very weak

Skills I would like to develop:

_____

_____

MY SOCIAL SELF

I like:
- [ ] most people
- [ ] many people
- [ ] some people
- [ ] a few people
- [ ] nobody

I have:
- [ ] many close friends
- [ ] some close friends
- [ ] a few close friends
- [ ] no close friends

My friends think I am:
- [ ] generous
- [ ] thoughtful
- [ ] hostile
- [ ] angry
- [ ] mean
- [ ] pleasant, kind
- [ ] undependable

I get along best with:
- [ ] my own age group
- [ ] people younger than I
- [ ] people older than I
- [ ] adults

	YES	NO
I cooperate with adults	[ ]	[ ]
I accept instructions with reluctance	[ ]	[ ]
I dislike my superiors	[ ]	[ ]
I rebel against authority	[ ]	[ ]
I compliment others frequently	[ ]	[ ]
I never compliment others	[ ]	[ ]
I never comment about others	[ ]	[ ]
I sometimes make fun of others	[ ]	[ ]
I often make fun of others	[ ]	[ ]
I am very accepting of others	[ ]	[ ]
I am sometimes critical	[ ]	[ ]
I am very critical	[ ]	[ ]

MY EMOTIONAL SELF

Most days I feel:
- [ ] bright and happy
- [ ] sad and gloomy
- [ ] neutral
- [ ] excited
- [ ] dull

I think I am usually:
- [ ] happy, pleasant
- [ ] hostile, angry
- [ ] kind, thoughtful
- [ ] mean
- [ ] silly
- [ ] cooperative
- [ ] irresponsible
- [ ] humorous
- [ ] friendly
- [ ] dependable
- [ ] polite

When I am happy, I _____
_____

When I am sad, I _____
_____

When I am angry, I _____
_____

When I am excited, I _____
_____

When I am depressed, I_____
_____

When I feel pressured, I_____
_____

When I hate, I _____
_____

When I fail, I_____
_____

MY SOCIAL SELF

(Grades 4-Adult/Ages 9 and up)

Objective:

To increase participants' self-understanding and social awareness by using the social self-evaluation sheet

Materials:

☐ Copy of *My Social Self* (page 135) and a pencil for each participant

Procedure:

Explain the importance of other people in our lives. Ask the participants the following question:

"Who sits around your dinner table?"

This question gives the group members a chance to reflect on their close relationships at home. Discuss how our first close relationships begin at home with our families and, as we grow older, we develop other close relationships with people we meet at social institutions such as school, clubs, etc. Then ask:

"Why is it important to have other people in our lives?"

Distribute a copy of *My Social Self* and a pencil to each participant. Tell the participants how much time they have to complete the activity sheet. When the allotted time has elapsed, begin a group discussion using the following questions:

- "What did you learn about yourself from this experience?"
  Example: I learned that I really prefer my own company to being around a lot of people.
- "What did you learn about yourself that you dislike?"
  Example: I dislike that my friends think I am bossy.
- "What can you change?"
  Example: I would like to work on not being so bossy by trying not to run everything.

If the group meets later, you may want to make a contract on the last question and set some definite goals for the last question.

Example: This week I would like to approach and talk to someone I don't know.

MY SOCIAL SELF

I like:

- [ ] most people I meet
- [ ] many people I meet
- [ ] some people I meet
- [ ] a few people I meet

I have:

- [ ] many close friends
- [ ] some close friends
- [ ] a few close friends
- [ ] no close friends

Most of my friends are:

- [ ] the same sex
- [ ] the opposite sex
- [ ] about equal of both

My close friends think I am:

- [ ] a great person
- [ ] OK
- [ ] a sorry person

I get to know people well:

- [ ] immediately
- [ ] gradually
- [ ] very slowly
- [ ] never

I am:

	YES	NO
Very accepting	[ ]	[ ]
Sometimes critical of people	[ ]	[ ]
Very critical most of the time	[ ]	[ ]
I think I am a leader	[ ]	[ ]
I think I am a follower	[ ]	[ ]
I think I am sometimes both	[ ]	[ ]

I get along best with:

- [ ] my own age group
- [ ] younger people
- [ ] older people
- [ ] adults
- [ ] older adults

	YES	NO
I cooperate with adults	[ ]	[ ]
I accept instructions	[ ]	[ ]
with reluctance	[ ]	[ ]
I dislike my superiors	[ ]	[ ]
I rebel against most authority	[ ]	[ ]

My friends think I am:

- [ ] bossy
- [ ] rude
- [ ] selfish
- [ ] cheerful
- [ ] courteous
- [ ] friendly
- [ ] generous
- [ ] gossipy
- [ ] truthful
- [ ] polite

	YES	NO
I compliment others readily	[ ]	[ ]
I never compliment others	[ ]	[ ]
I don't comment	[ ]	[ ]
I sometimes make	[ ]	[ ]
fun of others	[ ]	[ ]
I often make fun of others	[ ]	[ ]

GROUP COMMUNICATION

(Grades 4-Adult/Ages 9 and up)

Objective:

To assist group members in assessing their communication in the group

Materials:

☐ Copy of *Group Communication* (page 137) and a pencil for each participant

Procedure:

After a group has been in progress for some time, give the members an opportunity to assess their feelings and behavior in the group by using the *Group Communication* sheet. Distribute a copy of *Group Communication* and a pencil to each participant. Instruct the group members to read each statement and circle the word(s) or number that best describes their feelings about themselves. If necessary, explain how a continuum line works. Tell the participants how much time they have to complete the sheet. When the allotted time has elapsed, discuss any changes that could be made to make the group more satisfying for each member.

Examples of possible changes the group may want to make:

- Agree to be more careful at expressing reflective listening.
- Be more aware of body language and taking turns.
- Discuss ways of showing respect when people make suggestions.
- Investigate ways which the group members influence each other and ways which group members carry out suggestions made in the group.
- If a statement is scored below three for some people, discuss the ways these individual behaviors can affect group cooperation.
- Ask each member to share ways he/she has contributed to the group.
- Ask members to share ways other people in the group have contributed.
- Ask for contracts for changes for those who score themselves below three on a statement.
- Praise the work of the group and give specific commendations to each participant.

Conclude the session by asking:

"Overall what do you think has happened that has made this group effective? ineffective?"

Examples:

- We have all helped each other to do better in our school work.
- We have spent too much time arguing with each other about things that are unimportant.

GROUP COMMUNICATION

1. **I feel understood and listened to in this group.**

    1 · · · 2 · · · 3 · · · 4 · · · 5 · · · 6 · · · 7 · · · 8 · · · 9 · · · · 10
    NOT AT ALL   COMPLETELY

2. **I feel that I have considerable influence on group decisions.**

    1 · · · 2 · · · 3 · · · 4 · · · 5 · · · 6 · · · 7 · · · 8 · · · 9 · · · · 10
    NOT AT ALL   COMPLETELY

3. **I feel responsible and committed to the decisions made by the group.**

    1 · · · 2 · · · 3 · · · 4 · · · 5 · · · 6 · · · 7 · · · 8 · · · 9 · · · · 10
    NOT AT ALL   COMPLETELY

4. **I feel satisfied with my performance in the group.**

    1 · · · 2 · · · 3 · · · 4 · · · 5 · · · 6 · · · 7 · · · 8 · · · 9 · · · 10
    NOT AT ALL   COMPLETELY

5. **I feel that I have made a satisfactory contribution to the group.**

    1 · · · 2 · · · 3 · · · 4 · · · 5 · · · 6 · · · 7 · · · 8 · · · 9 · · · · 10
    NOT AT ALL   COMPLETELY

6. **I evaluate myself as being a good group member.**

    1 · · · 2 · · · 3 · · · 4 · · · 5 · · · 6 · · · 7 · · · 8 · · · 9 · · · · 10
    NOT AT ALL   COMPLETELY

WHAT IF?

(Grades 4-12/Ages 9-18)

Objective:

To assist participants in understanding character education by having them evaluate decisions

Materials:

☐ Copy of *What If?* (page 139) and a pencil for each participant

Procedure:

This is basically a values exercise. No judgments should be made as participants read and discuss their answers. It is a good time to put reflective listening skills to work both for the leader and the group participants.

Tell the participants:

> "I would like to have your honest answers concerning the following *What If's?* When everyone has completed the activity sheet, we will discuss as a group those situations which you found confusing or conflicting."

Distribute a copy of *What If?* and a pencil to each participant and allow time for them to complete the entire sheet. When they have completed the sheet, have each group member take a turn, sharing one response at a time. Remember the basic rule of the group is not to force participation. Remind the participants that they can say "I pass" if they do not wish to read an answer. As the leader, feel free to share what you would do in any of the situations. As the group members read their answers, you may ask questions such as:

- How did you decide on that approach?
- How do you see that working out for your best interest?
- How do you see that working out for the other party's best interest?
- What would be the possible consequences of taking that action?
- What could you change in the response that would change the consequences?

WHAT IF?

Read the following sentences and write what you would do in each situation.

1. Someone wants to throw a stone at the window of another person's house.
   I would _____ .

2. You break the pencil sharpener in your classroom, but no one saw you do it.
   I would _____ .

3. You get on the bus and the driver forgets to collect your fare.
   I would _____ .

4. Your team loses the game.
   I would _____ .

5. You get tired and want to go to bed before guests have left your home.
   I would _____ .

6. You find a purse and don't know who it belongs to.
   I would _____ .

7. A stranger stops and asks you to go to the circus with him/her.
   I would _____ .

8. You have two friends who don't get along with each other.
   I would _____ .

9. Your best friend makes unkind remarks about a new student in your class.
   I would _____ .

10. Your mother mentions that she never has time to do anything she likes to do.
    I would _____ .

11. Your grandmother lives alone and wants you to come over, but you had planned
    to go to a movie with a friend.
    I would _____ .

12. You see the girl across from you cheating on a test.
    I would _____ .

13. Your best friend wants to borrow your homework to get the answers.
    I would _____ .

14. Your dad gives you too much money for your school play costume.
    I would _____ .

MIRACLES

(Grades 4-Adult/Ages 9 and up)

Objective:

To increase the awareness of the special things which happen in participants' lives everyday

To increase participants' positive attitudes

Materials:

☐ Copy of *Miracles* (page 141) and a pencil for each participant

Procedure:

Ask the group members to define the word *miracle*. After some discussion, give the participants the following *Webster Dictionary* definition:

> "a wonderful thing, a surprise, a remarkable event which may defy the laws of scientific explanation."

Distribute a copy of *Miracles* and a pencil to each participant. Ask each group member to record any miracles which occur in their lives between now and the time they come back to the group. When the group next meets, provide an opportunity for the group members to share their miracles with each other.

MIRACLES

DATE		MIRACLE
____	1.	_____
____	2.	_____
____	3.	_____
____	4.	_____
____	5.	_____
____	6.	_____
____	7.	_____
____	8.	_____
____	9.	_____
____	10.	_____
____	11.	_____
____	12.	_____
____	13.	_____
____	14.	_____
____	15.	_____
____	16.	_____
____	17.	_____
____	18.	_____

RANK ORDER

(Grades 6-12/Ages 11-18)

Objective:

To raise participants' awareness and to inform leaders of concerns and needs of participants to be used for the purpose of program planning

Materials:

☐ Copy of the *Rank Order Sheet* (page 143) and a pencil for each participant and the leader

Procedure:

Distribute a copy of the *Rank Order Sheet* and a pencil to each participant. Instruct them to rank the items listed on the sheet in order of the seriousness of the problem for them personally. The most serious concern will be ranked #1, next serious #2, etc. When everyone has completed the activity sheet, the leader should read each statement aloud and tally the number of participants who ranked each statement #1-#5 in seriousness. A tally of these answers can give information to the group as well as to the leader in determining the need for subsequent sessions/programs.

This exercise can also be used to determine what topics need further discussion in a small-group setting. If most of the participants, for example, rank "Withstanding Peer Pressure" in the top five concerns, organize a group focusing on peer pressure or use a session of the current group to discuss the difficulties and advantages of peer pressure. This procedure can be followed with each of the group members' concerns.

Participants may also find comfort in finding out how many other people have their same concerns. For example, the concern of "Feeling Torn Between Too Many Activities" may lead the group members to discuss ways to balance their lives and present alternative ways of dealing with the stress of being overwhelmed. (See *Problem-Solving*, pages 92-94)

When the tally sheets indicate a high number of identical concerns, the leader can plan a series around that topic for classroom guidance or perhaps for an entire school emphasis.

RANK ORDER SHEET

- ☐ Communicating with parents
- ☐ Having to get good grades
- ☐ Making friends
- ☐ Dealing with family feuds
- ☐ Feeling left out with peers
- ☐ Dealing with bullies
- ☐ Withstanding peer pressure
- ☐ Making decisions in boy/girl relationships
- ☐ Feeling pressured with too much work
- ☐ Feeling torn between too many activities
- ☐ Believing that nobody is really listening
- ☐ Understanding and accepting death
- ☐ Being teased
- ☐ Being limited with time
- ☐ Being rejected
- ☐ Lacking self-confidence
- ☐ Being tempted to drink alcohol or take drugs
- ☐ Dealing with anger and frustration
- ☐ Being pressured to achieve
- ☐ Limited freedom in decision making
- ☐ Getting along with siblings
- ☐ Getting along with authority figures (teachers, parents)

PERSONAL TIME CAPSULES

(Grades 4-10/Ages 9-16)

Objective:

To identify participants' favorites and to raise the awareness that people change over a period of time

Materials:

☐ Copy of *My Favorites* (page 145), envelope, and a pencil for each participant

Procedure:

Distribute a copy of *My Favorites*, an envelope, and a pencil to each participant. Then read the following paragraph to the group members:

"Each of you is going to complete a list of favorites and store it away like a time capsule. These envelopes will hold your time capsules. In three months, (the leader needs to choose a reasonable amount of time depending on the availability of the group) we will open the envelopes to see how much information is still accurate. Fill out *My Favorites,* seal your envelope, and write your name and the date on the outside. The envelopes will be stored in a secret, safe place and returned to you at the end of the time period."

When the envelopes are returned to the participants, have them re-read the activity sheet and decide which things have remained their favorites and which are no longer their favorites. As a group, discuss why their responses changed or remained the same.

MY FAVORITES

Name _____ Date _____

Height _____ Weight _____

MY FAVORITE:

Friend _____

Song _____

Place _____

Color _____

TV show _____

Thing _____

Thing I want _____

Wish _____

Model (person I admire) _____

Activity _____

Game _____

Subject in school _____

Book _____

Movie _____

Career choice _____

Skill _____

Talent _____

PROFILE
(Grades 6-Adult/Ages 11 and up)

Objective:

To help participants gain insight and self-awareness by identifying characteristics which influence communication

Materials:

☐ Copy of *Profile* (page 147) and a pencil for each participant

Procedure:

Distribute a copy of *Profile* and a pencil to each participant and ask them to look carefully at the activity sheet. Then tell the group members to think carefully about the way they see themselves and about the way they think others see them as they decide where to mark each line. Instruct the participants to mark an ✕ on the continuum line to indicate the way they see themselves, and an O to indicate the way they think others see them. Explain that the marks they place on the continuum line should represent where they think they are in their self-development.

For example:

If they think they are a talker more than a listener, they would mark the continuum:

TALKER   I----I----I-✕-I----I----I----I----I----I----I   LISTENER

If they think others see them more as a listener, they would mark the continuum:

TALKER   I----I----I-✕-I----I----I----I-O-I----I----I----I   LISTENER

When everyone has completed the activity sheet, say:

"You may share as many of your answers with the group as you wish. The ✕'s will always remain where you have marked them, but if someone in our group sees you differently then your O mark indicates, we will take time to discuss the reason he/she believes this. If you agree with what the person says, you may move your O to a different place on the line. If you disagree with what the person is saying, you may want to find out why they feel differently. After hearing why they disagree, you may move your O to a different place on the line if you wish to do so."

PROFILE

TALKER |----|----|----|----|----|----|----|----|----|----| LISTENER

DOER |----|----|----|----|----|----|----|----|----|----| THINKER

PIONEER |----|----|----|----|----|----|----|----|----|----| SETTLER

TODAY |----|----|----|----|----|----|----|----|----|----| TOMORROW

SPENDER |----|----|----|----|----|----|----|----|----|---| SAVER

OPTIMIST |----|----|----|----|----|----|----|----|---|----| PESSIMIST

GIVER |----|----|----|----|----|----|----|----|----|----| RECEIVER

DEPENDENT |----|----|----|----|----|----|----|----|----|----| INDEPENDENT

RESPONDER |----|----|----|----|----|----|----|----|----|----| CONTROLLER

FAMILY

(Grades 4-12/Ages 9-18)

Objective:

To identify family feelings and influences on group members

Materials:

☐ Paper and crayons or colored pencils for each participant

Procedure:

Distribute a piece of paper and crayons or colored pencils to each participant. Instruct the group members to divide their paper into four parts by either drawing lines or folding the paper. Tell the group members that in each section they are to draw a symbol which represents their family for the following items: (If necessary, discuss the meaning if the word *symbol* and give several examples.)

1. Flag
2. Animal
3. Plant
4. Object (dollar bill, key, coin, geometric figure)

When everyone has finished drawing, give each person a chance to share the meaning of their symbols in each square. Dividing the participants into small groups or partners may facilitate the use of time.

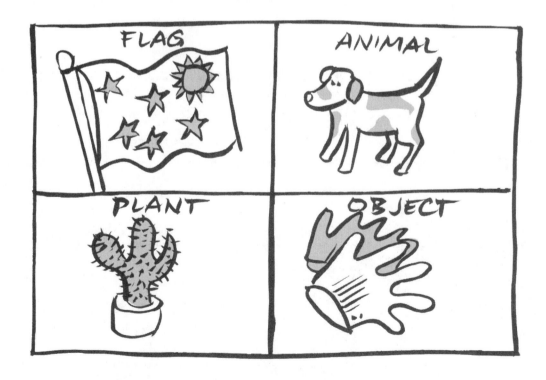

TOOLS FOR

CAREER AWARENESS

WHAT DO YOU WANT TO DO?

(Grades 6-12/Ages 11-18)

Objective:

To help participants develop career awareness by identifying jobs and interests

Materials:

- ☐ Chalkboard and chalk or flipchart and marker
- ☐ Paper and a pencil for each participant

Procedure:

Ask the group members to name as many different jobs and careers as possible and list them on the chalkboard/flipchart. Distribute a piece of paper and a pencil to each participant. Then instruct the group members to write the answers to the following questions on their papers.

- What do you like to do most?
- What do you like to do for fun?
- What things do you do best?
- Where do you like to live?
- What type person are you?
    - Are you more fun-loving or serious?
    - Are you more talkative or thinking?
    - Are you more indoors or outdoors?

Ask for a few volunteers to share their answers to the above questions with the group. Write their responses on the chalkboard/flipchart. Have the group members match the personal qualities of the volunteers with the jobs listed on the board. Then have them match their own personal qualities with the job list.

CAREER CONSEQUENCES CARDS

(Grades 3-8/Ages 8-13)

Objective:

To increase participants' awareness of the names of careers and career attributes and facts

To associate school subjects with careers

Materials:

☐ Fifty 3" x 5" cards with one statement (page 153) written on each card (if playing as a card game with verbal responses)

Procedure:

Determine whether the game will be played individually or in teams and whether players will give written or verbal answers.

If the responses are to be given verbally, place the cards face-down in a pile. Have one person begin by drawing the first card from the pile, reading the statement aloud, and giving his/her response. Continue the game having each player take a turn by drawing a card and responding. A point is given for each correct answer. The player with the highest score wins.

If the responses are to be written, the leader should read each statement aloud to the group. The group members should write their answers as individuals or play in teams with a selected team member recording the groups' answer to each statement. After all the cards have been read and answered, check the answers as a group. A point is given for each correct answer. The player/team with the highest score wins.

The learning value of this exercise will be increased if there is discussion at given intervals about the relationship of jobs to subjects studied at school.

Note: You may add to this list on page 153 as extensively as you desire to increase the stack of cards. This can be a good game for participants to play if they finish their work early.

1. Name 2 tools a carpenter uses in his work.
2. Name 3 things a nurse does.
3. Name 4 things a police officer does.
4. Name 2 things a school principal does.
5. Name 4 things a trash collector does.
6. Name 2 dangers a coal miner faces.
7. Name 3 things an veterinarian must know.
8. Name 4 tools a mechanic uses in his work.
9. Name 3 things a school counselor does.
10. Name 2 occupations where driving is necessary.
11. Name 3 life-threatening dangerous jobs.
12. Name 4 things a homemaker does.
13. Name 2 things you like most about what a professional athlete does.
14. Name 3 things you would like about being a gardener.
15. Name 2 kinds of special clothing a fire fighter uses.
16. Name 4 jobs that might use mathematics.
17. Name 3 jobs where pencils might be used.
18. Name 5 jobs which require the use of computers.
19. Name 3 jobs where a FAX machine is important.
20. Name 3 reasons a ship captain needs to know geography.
21. Name 3 jobs where it is important to be friendly.
22. Name 4 jobs which you think you might like.
23. Name 2 jobs where you might get lonely.
24. Name 3 jobs where people work alone.
25. Name 4 jobs that require creative talent.
26. Name 4 jobs that are done inside.
27. Name 4 jobs that are done outside.
28. Name 4 jobs that are good for persons wanting summer work.
29. Name 3 things you have learned in school which will help you get a job.
30. Name 5 subjects in school that help you in a job.
31. Name 4 jobs that require a knowledge of business.
32. Name 4 kinds of jobs that require selling.
33. Name 3 kinds of places where you need to know video production.
34. Name 3 jobs that require mechanical ability.
35. Name 4 jobs that require a knowledge of color.
36. Name 3 jobs where your body size makes a difference.
37. Name 2 jobs where it is important to have a small body.
38. Name 3 jobs where physical strength is necessary.
39. Name 3 jobs where it is important to be physically fit.
40. Name 4 jobs that require excellent speaking skills.
41. Name 4 jobs that have no schedule (flexible hours).
42. Name 3 jobs that require teaching ability.
43. Name 6 jobs that are seen as "helping" careers.
44. Name 3 jobs related to nature.
45. Name 3 jobs requiring a knowledge of animals.
46. Name 3 jobs that require brushes.
47. Name 3 jobs that require scissors.
48. Name 5 jobs that require leadership ability.
49. Name 3 jobs where ladders are important.
50. Name 3 jobs that require going up high (above the ground).

PEOPLE WHO WORK IN OUR SCHOOL

(Grades 3-5/Ages 8-10)

Objective:

To increase participants' awareness of careers and what people do in the school

Materials:

☐ Chalkboard and chalk or flipchart and marker
☐ Copy of *Interview Sheet* (page 155) and a pencil for each interviewer

Procedure:

Make arrangements to walk through the building and observe all the people who work in the school. After returning to the classroom, list on the chalkboard/flipchart all the jobs which are available in the building. In addition to all the professional personnel, do not forget the service people who come into the building from time to time such as heating repairpersons, plumbers, and window washers. Discuss with the participants the training and duties which each job requires. Next, compile a list of questions about various jobs.

For example:

- What is your most important duty on your job?
- What kind of training do you need for your job?
- What kind of personality works best on your job?
- What motivated you to choose this job?
- Would you recommend this job to others as a career? Why?
- What do you do each day that you most enjoy?
- What do you do that you dislike?
- Would you want to do this job for the rest of your life?
- In what way does your job involve other people?
- What is the most stressful thing about your job?
- What is the most disappointing thing about your job?
- What is the most exciting thing about your job?
- What about your job would you change if you could?
- What about your job do you always want to stay the same?

Ask for volunteers to interview the people on the list who are easily accessible. Set up a time or tell the students to arrange a time to interview the person. Distribute a copy of the *Interview Sheet* and a pencil to each interviewer. Help the interviewers select only appropriate questions from the sheet so they do not take too much time from the person being interviewed.

When the interviews have been completed, have the students write a summary about each job and put it in a booklet entitled "People Who Work In Our School." Students could also draw a picture of each person to add interest to the book.

INTERVIEW SHEET

JOB TITLE _____

NAME OF PERSON BEING INTERVIEWED _____

1. What is your most important duty on your job? _____
   _____

2. What kind of training do you need for your job? _____
   _____

3. What kind of personality works best on your job? _____
   _____

4. What motivated you to choose this job? _____
   _____

5. Would you recommend this job to others as a career? _____
   Why?_____

6. What do you do each day that you most enjoy? _____
   _____

7. What do you do that you dislike? _____
   _____

8. Would you want to do this job for the rest of your life? _____
   _____

9. In what way does your job involve other people? _____
   _____

10. What is the most stressful thing about your job? _____
    _____

11. What is the most disappointing thing about your job? _____

12. What is the most exciting thing about your job? _____
    _____

13. What about your job would you change if you could? _____
    _____

14. What about your job do you always want to stay the same? _____
    _____

ADDITIONAL QUESTIONS:

_____
_____
_____
_____

YOUR RESUMÉ
(Grades 6-12/Ages 11-18)

Objective:

To help participants gain awareness about themselves and to encourage writing this information in an organized manner

To foster opportunities for better understanding in a group setting

Materials:

- ☐ 2 pieces of paper and a pencil for each participant

Procedure:

Distribute two pieces of paper and a pencil to each participant. Explain that the purpose of a resumé is to communicate information about themselves to another person. It is a reflection of themselves, their personality, creativity, and ability to express these thoughts.

Instruct the participants to informally write in their own words how they see themselves and how they want others to see them. As they are completing their informal paper, write the following information on the chalkboard/flipchart:

- Full name _____
- Address _____
- Telephone _____
- Educational background _____
- Languages spoken_____
- Special skills _____
- Life or employment objectives _____
- Hobbies or special interests _____

When the participants have completed the informal papers, tell them to rewrite the informal paper in a formal manner being sure to include any information, such as those things listed on the chalkboard/flipchart, that would be important to an employer or an organization when applying for position/membership.

Alternatives:

Ask the participants share their resumés with the group. After five resumés have been presented, ask the participants how many facts they can remember about each presenter. This can be repeated after each group of five presentations. This activity will encourage listening skills. If the participants write down the things they remembered, recognize the person who most accurately remembered the information presented.

JOURNALIST
(Grades 3-Adult/Ages 8 and up)

Objective:

To encourage news writing, provide participants ways of sharing personal stories, and to encourage creativity

Materials:

☐ Sheet of newsprint and magic marker for each participant

Procedure:

Distribute a sheet of newsprint and magic marker to each participant. Announce that each person is going to design a newspaper. The name of the paper will be based on the first or last name of the journalist writing the paper. For example: Joey's Journal, Hester's Herald, Cecilia's Constitution. The newspaper titles should be euphonic so participants will enjoy the sound of the title.

Instruct each person to write three stories about something important that has happened to him/her over a certain appointed period of time.

For example:

- In January: Write three stories about something that happened in the past year.
- In September: Write three stories about something that happened during the past summer.
- At the end of the quarter: Write three stories about the last quarter.
- In June: Write stories about the last school year.

Instruct the group members to design their newspapers and write their stories. When everyone has completed his/her newspaper, have the participants share their stories with the group. Have them discuss:

- Similar stories
- Unique stories
- Scary stories
- Exciting stories
- Adventurous stories
- Humorous stories

This is an excellent activity to use with adults who are returning after a period of absence—faculties at the end of summer, or convention groups who see each other once a year.

EVALUATION

Date _____/_____/_____

This group experience has been …

☐ Very meaningful   ☐ Passable   ☐ Ineffective   ☐ Helpful

I most liked _____
_____
_____

I learned or relearned _____
_____
_____

I would change _____

Other comments _____
_____
_____
_____

EVALUATION

Date _____/_____/_____

This group experience has been …

☐ Very meaningful   ☐ Passable   ☐ Ineffective   ☐ Helpful

I most liked _____
_____
_____

I learned or relearned _____
_____
_____

I would change _____

Other comments _____
_____
_____
_____

ABOUT THE AUTHOR

Mary Joe Hannaford, now deceased, worked as a private consultant, trainer, and speaker on counseling related subjects. She was formerly the coordinator of the counseling department in the Gwinnett Public Schools near Atlanta, Georgia, where she originated the elementary counseling program as well as coordinated the middle and high school programs. The counselors in her department have received many state and national awards with over seventeen of them being named Counselor of the Year by the American School Counselor Association. Mary Joe personally received the American School Counselor Coordinator of the Year Award in addition to Writer of the Year for her book, *Counselors Under Construction*.

ABOUT THE ARTIST

Joey Hannaford has been a professional calligrapher and graphic designer for twelve years, with her own studio in the Atlanta area for the last six of those years. With a BFA in Graphic Design and a MFA in Printmaking with research in papermaking from the University of Georgia, she is uniquely qualified to cross the boundaries of these varied disciplines with her work.